Classic Restaurants
OF
MICHIANA

Classic Restaurants

OF

MICHIANA

Jane Simon Ammeson

AMERICAN PALATE

Published by American Palate
A Division of The History Press
Charleston, SC
www.historypress.com

First published 2023

Manufactured in the United States

ISBN 9781467152518

Library of Congress Control Number: 2023940756

To my husband, John Fields; my son, Evan Ammeson, and his life partner, Emily Kowerduck; and my daughter, Nia Ammeson.

CONTENTS

"Fenetta L" of Indian Beach

Named after the wife of W.E. Tuttle, the *Fenetta L* was built in 1901 and operated out of Tuttle's Landing on Indian Lake. *North Berrien Historical Museum*.

PREFACE

I am writing this while trying to make a deadline, surrounded by old advertisements, articles and photographs towering in piles and folders that are threatening to cascade down all around me. There are piles and piles that I desperately want to include—it seems like every time I learn of a new old restaurant or hotel or popular food that is no longer in our culinary lexicon (Chicken in the Rough anyone?), I want to include it or do more research, which sends me down a rabbit hole where I find even more that I want to add. That in turn sends me down—well, you get the idea.

Surely, I think, readers will want to know about the Silver Tower and Lido in South Bend or Zeke's in Dowagiac. But how to include everything I've learned about food and restaurants in Michiana? But my editor and all the great people at The History Press keep sending me emails to (nicely) remind me there are such things as deadlines.

And so I am, with deep regrets, possibly missing some places, people and food.

When I started researching and writing, I hoped to accomplish two things.

The first is as an homage to all the restaurants, diners, taverns and stagecoach stops that once were but are no longer. Secondly, I see this as a guide and celebration of what remains. I want people to know that you can dine at the Volcano in South Bend, one of the first restaurants in the United States to serve a new dish called pizza. I want to show how you can pull up to the Old Tavern Inn in Sumnerville (Niles) and enter a place that has been

Above: According to shadowlandonsilverbeach. blog (Elizabeth Hamilton), the name Silver Beach was coined by Maude Schlenker while she was walking with her fiancé, Logan Drake, on a moonlit stroll on this stretch of sand just south of the St. Joseph River. Schlenker said the water "shimmered like silver." *The Tichnor Brothers Collection, Boston Public Library.*

Left: South Bend was home to at least two A&W Root Beer Barrels, giant barrels selling frosty mugs filled with root beer and root beer floats through their walk-up windows. One was located at the southeast corner of U.S. 31 and Ireland Road, another stood on Western Avenue and the third was on North Main Street in Elkhart. *The History Museum.*

Hunt's in Coloma was a place to get sandwiches and beverages. *North Berrien Historical Society.*

in business since Andrew Jackson was president. I want to take you to out-of-the-way places, like the Grand Junction in Benton Harbor; the Riverside Inn in Riverside, Michigan; the Get Away in Bridgman; Gala-tan's in Hartford; Martha's Midway Inn in South Bend; the View Tavern in South Bend; and Simeri's Old Town Tap, also in South Bend, to praise the decades-old heritage of these places that frankly don't impress from the outside but, inside, are all about great food in a warm and convivial atmosphere.

Let's visit together—in either spirit (by reading my book) or happenstance—such favorites as Tosi's Restaurant in Stevensville, Michigan, that started off as an Italian resort back in the 1920s, and D'Agostino's Navajo Bar and Grille, which once was called the Navajo Trading Post and featured a lion (a live one) named Jerry more than eighty years ago. Enjoy the view of the lake at Grand Mere Inn in Stevensville, a second-generation family fine-dining place that replaced the popular Ritter's more than forty years ago.

Did you know you can eat like a Studebaker (not the car but the family) at the wonderfully grand Tippecanoe Place in South Bend, a historic manse and former home of the Studebaker family? Sip wine at Saint Julian in Paw Paw, the oldest winery in Michigan and the first to hire a woman wine maker. And while you're in Paw Paw, enjoy an Italian meal at La Cantina, also family owned, that opened in 1936. Travel farther east, just a few miles away, to Tea Pot Dome, a dot in the road that is now considered part of Paw

Left: The Galat-Inn Restaurant and Lounge statue in Hartford, Michigan. *John Margolies Roadside America Photograph Archive (1972–2008).*

Below: Tosi's Restaurant in Stevensville. *Tosi's Restaurant.*

Opposite: The Tippecanoe Place in South Bend is a gourmet restaurant located in the old Studebaker Mansion built by Clem Studebaker between 1886 and 1889. Also on site now is the Studebaker Brewing Company. *Jane Simon Ammeson.*

Paw, and enter the diner with the same name. Yes, it opened in the 1920s, but who knows how either the place or the café got its name. After all the, the Tea Pot Dome scandal that almost brought down the Warren Harding presidency was an oil well in Wyoming.

Have you ever eaten at a place named after a fishing lure? Check out the Wounded Minnow in Dowagiac.

Think Italian at Macri's and Sunny's in South Bend, and if you liked the movie *Rudy*, check out Corby's Irish Pub, where scenes were filmed. Parisi's near the Notre Dame campus was a favorite of the university's late president Reverend Theodore Martin Hesburgh, CSC, and once he was too old and frail to visit, the restaurant sent his favorite meals to him. DiMaggio's in Coloma opened in the 1930s and is still family owned.

Let's grab a milkshake and burger at old-time drive-ins, like Mikey's in Bridgman, Bonnie Doon in South Bend, Carlson's in Michigan City, Eddie's Drive-in West in Coloma and Lutz's in Dowagiac, or eat one indoors at Redamak's in New Buffalo, the North Shore Inn in Benton Harbor, Tom and Lin's Kitchenette in South Bend and the Ritz Klub Tavern in Michigan City. Oh, and let's not forget the Welcome Inn in downtown Stevensville, which opened in the 1930s and is notable for its classic—and original—neon sign.

A fond look at what was the Ellinee Resort on Paw Paw Lake. *Benton Harbor Public Library.*

Bonnie Doon Drive-In in South Bend. This favorite ice cream place still has one location open in South Bend. *The History Museum.*

The House of David Hotel was another haunt of Capone and his gang. *Benton Harbor Public Library*.

Plank's Letterhead Circa 1889   *Courtesy John E. Owen Collection*

John O. Plank owned Plank's Hotel in St. Joseph, as well as several other luxury hotels. Plank's is a replica of the one surviving Plank-owned hotel, the lovely Grand Hotel on Mackinac Island. *St. Joseph Public Library*.

And while we can't eat at the original Plank's, which once stood majestically above Lake Michigan in Saint Joseph (it burned to the ground in 1898), we can dine at Plank's, the restaurant at Harbor Shores Resort on the Saint Joseph River, not far from where the original once stood. It was designed in homage to that wonderful old place.

There are old restaurants that still seem new—I'm talking to you, Anne Reitz, the owner of Caffe Tosi's in downtown Saint Joseph, which opened more than thirty years ago but seems just yesterday. And there are new places that seem like they've been around forever because they're comfortable and the staff and owners are so accommodating—here's to you, Brian Maynard and Forte, with locations in historic places, including the former Gillespie's Drugstore also in downtown Saint Joseph, where there was a soda fountain long ago, and the arts district in Benton Harbor in a building dating to the 1800s.

MICHIANA IS A SPECIAL place, encompassing Southwest Michigan and Northern Indiana. It's attracted the famous—and the infamous (we're talking about you, Al Capone)—through the years, lured here by the shoreline towns of Lake Michigan; the inland lakes, where resorts sprouted

The very grand Hotel St. Joseph with Plank's Tavern-on-the-Beach featured a wide wrap-around veranda, boat livery and bathhouses and was perched on the north side of the St. Joseph River. Built in 1889, it was destroyed in a fire in July 1898 and was never rebuilt. *St. Joseph Public Library.*

Southwest Michigan was known as the fruitbelt, a marketing term that brought visitors to partake in the area's plentiful fruit harvests. For fifty cents, you could take an hour-long ride through the orchards in "Brown's Big Car." *The Tichnor Brothers Collection, Boston Public Library.*

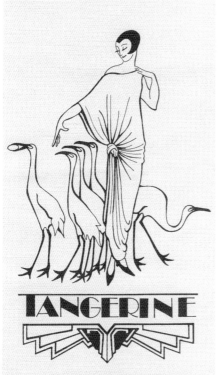

Above: The interior of the Moderne Restaurant in South Bend, Indiana. The Kalamaros family ran the restaurant for forty years before selling it in 1967. *The History Museum.*

Left: Located at 717 Michigan Avenue in LaPorte, Tangerine was an elegant restaurant that was open in the city's downtown area prior to the turn of this century. *Laporte County Historical Society.*

up starting in the late 1800s; the beauty of the Notre Dame campus; the numerous orchards brimming with fruit; and the rolling hills dotted with wineries (and now distilleries and breweries as well). The Saint Joseph River flows throughout Michiana, bringing with it the history of the Natives and the early French explorers.

ALSO PART OF THE area's multicultural fabric are the Eastern and Western Europeans—think of people from countries like Greece, Spain, France, Germany, Sweden, Poland, Hungary and more—and Black and Latino people who all work to make this place their home, leaving their culinary imprint along the way.

Food, history, the bounty of the land and water and people created a richness here. But that's just the past. Play it forward for there's always more to come. Read this book from cover to cover or dabble here and there. Look for what remains and what tempts your taste and hit the road, for this is a guide as well as a history.

So, think fondly at what once was—we regret never getting to feast on an ice cream sundae at the Moderne in South Bend; sip tea at Robertson's Department Store, also in South Bend; order a cocktail at the Tangerine in LaPorte; or sup at the Gas Light in Dowagiac.

But there are feasts waiting to be had, and this book is not only a remembrance but a way forward.

Jane Simon Ammeson

ACKNOWLEDGEMENTS

M ajor events are covered by newspapers, magazines, history books and, now, the internet. But it's shared memories, libraries, museums and social media that preserve the little-known facts about what we eat and where we eat. So, for everyone who posts on Facebook, Instagram and Twitter about a meal or the remembrance of a place they once loved to dine that is no longer there, keep in mind that you are, in a very special way, recording history.

And the same goes for those who donate to regional and local museums. How else would I have ever seen old menus, photographs and the like from restaurants and hotels?

So, a big thank-you is owed to all who helped me with this book. Because really, this couldn't have been done without all their tireless efforts to preserve history.

Here's a start, and if I've left anyone out, it's not because they didn't provide vital help—it's because I sometimes lose things in my towering piles of notes:

Danielle Adams, director, La Porte County Historical Society
Steve Arseneau, director, Dowagiac Area History Museum
Travis Childs, director of education and Saint Joseph County historian, the History Museum
Peter Cook, director of programs and outreach, North Berrien Historical Society
Savannah Jackson, assistant director, La Porte County Historical Society

Bruce R. Johnson, county historian, La Porte County Historical Society

Carole Kiernan, manager of visitor services, North Berrien Historical Society

Lincoln Township Public Library

Candace Myers, historian

Robert Myers, director of history programming, Historical Society of Michigan

Jill Rauh, reference and adult services librarian, Benton Harbor Public Library

Saint Joseph Public Library

Chris Siriano

I would also like to thank the countless people who shared their food and restaurant memories with me.

A special thanks to my editor John Rodrigue and Ashley Hill as well as everyone else at The History Press who work so hard to make my books turn out. I'm sorry for all the missed deadlines.

1
STAGECOACH STOPS

Andrew Jackson was president of the United States, and Michigan had just recently been granted statehood when Peabody Cook and his wife, Eliza, built a tavern and stage stop in Sumnerville in 1836.

Mrs. Cook was known for her cookery, and one of her specialties was her codfish balls, which a frequent visitor described as tasting like peaches and cream almost eighty years later, according to a news article that ran in the *Niles Star* and was discovered by the author of *Living History's Mysteries*.

To make her codfish balls, Mrs. Cook would have first ordered the codfish. Since there was no overnight delivery in refrigerated cargo containers back then—or even refrigeration—once the fish were caught in the waters of the Atlantic Ocean, they were beheaded, their insides removed, and then they were packed about eight hundred per barrel, with each layer being covered in salt. It was such an effective way to preserve the fish that, according to mountvernon.org, an archaeological investigation in 1991 of the cargo of a sailing vessel that sank in 1830 showed that some of the fish packed using this method remained edible. But no, I wasn't going to try any if offered.

The barrels weighed about 250 pounds and once filled with fish and cooks like Eliza would need to unpack them, wash away the salt, pick out the bones and then mash the fish along with cooked potatoes. But wait, she wasn't done yet. Then the mashed fish and potatoes were formed into balls and fried in lard. How this could even begin to taste similar to peaches and cream is hard to fathom, but it may be that the diners at Mrs. Cook's table were imbibing the whiskey Mr. Cook distilled and sold for three cents a

Left: Old Tavern Inn is often considered the oldest continuously operating business in Michigan. It has always operated in the same building. *Jane Simon Ammeson.*

Below: Cars line the road at Jean Klock Park in Benton Harbor. Jean Klock is one of the premier beaches in the area. *The Tichnor Brothers Collection, Boston Public Library.*

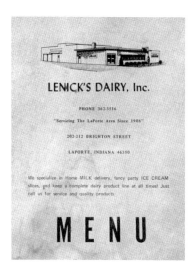

The cover of Lenick's menu. *LaPorte County Historical Society.*

dipper. That, of course, meant everyone was drinking out of the same dipper, but no one seems to have cared about sanitation back then when an overnight at a stage stop might mean three strangers were sleeping in the same bed.

You can still go to Peabody's, but now it's known as the Old Tavern Inn, and the last time I was there, I didn't see codfish balls on the menu. Instead, it's now a great place to get a cheeseburger and is recognized by the State of Michigan as the oldest business in Michigan still operating in its original building.

But the weathered building, a popular stopping place, isn't the oldest site in town.

Four thousand years ago, the Hopewell Native tribe built at least nine burial mounds, large slopping hills covered with grass that could easily be mistaken for just a slight bump in the landscape. Native mounds were common, but most were plowed over by farmers, and the land planted with crops. But the residents of Cass County did something unusual back then—they let the mounds remain, recognizing that they were sacred to the Native.

Stagecoach stops were the original restaurants and hotels in early America. The journeys were over horrid roads that were, at times, slogs of mud so deep from rainwater or snowmelt after the winter that passengers were ordered to get out and push. The reverse was true when dry weather turned roadbeds into dust and the wind and movement of the horses kicked up clouds of earth thick enough to choke—well, a horse. As if that wasn't bad enough, consider the coach wheels were made of wood and so were the seats inside. Nor was there air conditioning or heat. It's a wonder anyone traveled at all. But they did, and stagecoach stops were needed for changing and/or feeding and watering horses, and they were places where passengers could eat or even spend the night.

Harriet Martineau, an English woman who arrived in the United States in 1834, traveled throughout the country for the next two years. She traveled by stagecoach and whatever other means available as she visited the East Coast, the southern states and the Midwest. A self-trained sociologist who is credited with helping develop the field, she had an amazing interest in

EMERY RESORT ON RIVER BANK, ST. JOSEPH, MICH.

In 1895, N.C. Emery built a large addition to his residence and hotel Emery Resort on the St. Joseph River and enlarged the kitchen. He said he expected a lot more boarders and boaters, particularly those from Chicago, to stay. *Benton Harbor Public Library.*

Beach attire was certainly different back in the early days of Silver Beach as a destination. It's hard to imagine it was much fun sitting in the sand in long skirts and big hats. But this was the age where women could be arrested for wearing bathing suits that showed their knees. *The Tichnor Brothers Collection, Boston Public Library.*

everything around her and the fortitude typical of an English woman who loved to travel. At a stage stop in Niles, Michigan, Martineau wrote in her book, "The prairie strawberries, at breakfast this morning, were so large, sweet, and ripe, that we were inclined for more in the course of the day."

But alas, though Martineau observed many of the children of the settlers gathering strawberries in baskets, they wouldn't sell them to the travelers, fearful of what their mothers would say if they went home without berries for their fathers to eat. "Our driver observed that money was 'no object to them,'" continued Martineau in her narrative. "I began to think that we had, at last, got to the end of the world; or rather, perhaps, to the beginning of another and a better one."

Along with stagecoach stops, families often opened their homes to travelers, charging them for meals and beds to sleep in. Think of it like this—a car full of strangers pulls up to your home, and you invite them in to dine for a charge. That's similar to what Martineau experienced in Michigan City, Indiana, a port city on Lake Michigan, just across the border from Michigan. There, she and her fellow travelers ate at the home

The Bay Tree Inn, located at 902 Michigan Avenue, was the home of the Woman's Association, whose purpose it was to provide a center for the civic and social improvement of women and to maintain an educational and philanthropic enterprise. It had a dining room that was open to the public and was known for its macaroni and cheese. *LaPorte County Historical Society*.

of a widow. "Our supper of young pork, good bread, potatoes, preserves, and tea was served at two tables, where the gentlemen were in proportion to the ladies as ten to one," she writes. "In such places, there is a large proportion of young men who are to go back for wives when they have gathered a few other comforts about them."

It also turned out to be a handy place in other—sometimes more macabre—ways.

Daniel and Susan Dodge owned the only tavern in the newly established village of Paw Paw, Michigan. And when Susan died on November 9, 1836, she earned the sad distinction as the first person in the new community to pass away. Unfortunately, there was no cemetery in the village yet. The solution? Bury her behind the tavern. She wouldn't be the last. A sickness spread through Paw Paw that winter and spring, and over the next eighteen months, Susan was joined by other villagers. As for what happened to their bodies after a cemetery was establsihed, history is unclear.

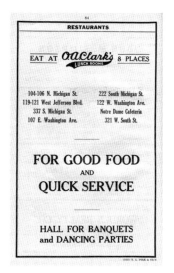

O.A. Clark's Lunch Rooms were founded by restaurateur Olen A. Clark, and by 1925, there were eight locations. The main restaurant and its office were located at 104 North Michigan Street, now the site of Café Navarre. Although Clark died in 1937, the lunchrooms remained open until the 1950s. *The History Museum.*

THE RASSETTE HOUSE WAS one of the first hotels in Hartford, and it was a stage stop as well. According to the *Tri County Record* (posted online), though the Rassette had a taproom where thirsty citizens could get a drink, for a while, the bar was run by a man who was a teetotaler. Since he didn't believe imbibing was a good thing, as the evenings wore on, he took it upon himself to water down men's drinks, causing one old-timer to say they'd be more likely to drown from consuming all that water than getting drunk.

Travel by stagecoach, aside from being uncomfortable, could be dangerous as well, and passengers were more than just customers paying for the ride. Using a four-horse hitch, Jacob Crager, who ran the stage line between Hartford and Paw Paw, left Hartford at 2:00 p.m. daily, returning the next day at 11:00 a.m.—or at least that was the plan. One pretty fall day, Crager flicked his whip to get the horses going. His coach, filled with passengers and bags of mail, left the front of the Rassette, headed for Paw Paw, a little

Chautauquas were days-long events that occurred around the turn of the last century until around the 1930s, when they had to compete with movie shows, vaudeville acts and, soon after, television. But in their time, they were well attended by people interested in hearing educational lectures, singing and musical performances by groups like Cleaver's Gypsy Quintet. The tents erected were large, capable of holding several thousand people at a time. The ladies, dressed in white, shown in the photograph on page 53 of the Fairview Hotel, were said to be there to visit the chautauquas held each year in South Bend and Mishawaka. Some would last five to seven days. The Honorable Teddy Roosevelt spoke at the South Bend Chautauqua in 1915 and Willian Jennings Bryan two years after that. *LaPorte County Historical Society.*

The Krieger house stood at the corner of Port and Main Streets. It later became the Riverview Hotel and was torn down in the 1960s. *St. Joseph Public Library.*

31

over fourteen miles away. But three miles down the road, in a wooded area, the horses were spooked and bolted, and in their wild rush to get away from what scared them (and it doesn't take much to scare a horse), the animals dragged the stage down a sand bank toward a lake. With no road service to call, the passengers had to disembark and assist in pushing the vehicle back onto the road. There, they patched up a broken wheel and continued on, but when they reached Paw Paw, there was no supper to be had.

There were three classes of passengers, according to a joke back then, and three rates of fare: first, second and third class. All the passengers rode in the same coach, but when a mud hole was reached, first-class passengers remained seated, second-class passengers were ordered to get out and walk and third-class passengers had to get out and push.

When the mud was deep, many foot travelers ended up barefoot after their shoes and boots got stuck. A tale was told of a Saint Joseph boy who was traveling home on foot when he became mired in mud so deep that only his head was above the mud. Responding to his cries for help, neighbors came and pulled him out. But he said he had to go back to get his boots; otherwise, his dad would give him Jericho. (I'm taking it Jericho wasn't a good thing.)

Nowadays, we're used to the conformity of chain hotels and restaurants, but each stop for those wanting a drink, a meal or a place to stay varied according to the owner.

Consider Grandma Teeter, who, with her husband, Van Buren, operated the Teeter House, a stagecoach stop in Hartford, Michigan. She then decided to add to her earnings by selling squabs to the fancy restaurants nearby. To accomplish this, she removed the windows in one of the building's bedrooms and added shelves for the birds, including pigeons and doves, to roost. "But," recalled her granddaughter Gladys Guy Andrews, "she was too kind-hearted to kill or eat any of them."

So, we're imagining a room full of birds and their poo.

Grandma Teeter was a force of nature. She not only helped run the hotel, but she was also a baby nurse and midwife, a service so valuable that many locals relied on her expertise, some stating they couldn't have a baby without her in attendance.

Starting around 1831, Pitt Brown ran a ferry that took people across the broad Saint Joseph River. He soon became the first postmaster in Saint Joseph. He operated out of his house, where he later established a distillery.

Early taverns were built of logs and typically had just a few rooms, the largest being the bar. If there were too many guests, the men would sleep

Note the buffet sign on the left side of this photograph taken in downtown Benton Harbor. *St. Joseph Public Library.*

The American House, on the corner of Main and Pipestone, was one of the earliest hotels in the St. Joseph–Benton Harbor area. When Edgar Nichols was proprietor there, George Harley was the bartender, and four waitresses were needed to serve patrons. *St. Joseph Public Library.*

A very early view of Hotel Benton, when horses still ruled. *Benton Harbor Public Library*.

on the floor—some probably couldn't make it much farther anyway. On a positive note, the food was generally plentiful and filling but plain. There were stews, soups, beans, huge roasts of wild game and immense loaves of bread that the host would carve into large chunks and hand out as guests called for them. Diners used these hunks to soak up the grease and gravy from their plates or even from the platters on which the food was served. Coffee and tea were such luxuries that they weren't usually served; instead, patrons drank home-brewed beer or ale.

Israel and Rose Hess owned a stop on a stagecoach route located on U.S. 33, just south of Goshen near County Road 40 in Elkhart County. What is now U.S. 33 was once known as the Fort Wayne Road and was a route used by the stagecoach operating between Goshen and Fort Wayne. This route would have been important, especially since Fort Wayne was the closest banking town. It is said some of the rooms in the house were named after stops on the stagecoach route. The house still stands but is now a private residence.

Historian Robert Myers, who has written numerous articles and books on early Berrien County, says that meals would consist of what could be foraged and hunted, bought or traded with the Natives, who grew corn and beans, among other food items. Soon, pioneers were growing food on their own farms, which sprang up around the major cities like South Bend and Saint Joseph.

Hotel Benton in Benton Harbor. *Benton Harbor Public Library.*

According to the North Berrien Historical Museum, when the interurban ceased operations to the Coloma, Ernest Erickson, the owner of the Ellinee, a resort on Paw Paw Lake, knew that would negatively impact his business, so he opted to create his own transportation and developed his own bus line. *North Berrien Historical Museum.*

Chickens would have run loose in the yards before they were scooped up, beheaded, plucked and fried in lard. But these were stringy birds that lived on bugs and grasses, not fattened on grain. The same went for the plentiful wild turkeys. Corn was tough and best eaten when green, as people often lost their teeth early and had to gum it. When it grew yellow, it wasn't sweet like we enjoy it now; instead, it was tough and given to animals to eat.

Wild game and birds, including grouse, doves, partridges, beavers, muskrats, racoons and the occasional bear that still roamed the woods and beaches, might have been thrown into a big iron cauldron along with root vegetables, such as carrots, potatoes, squash and whatever else was available, and onions and ramps—those garlicky tasting greens that grew in big clumps. Water would be poured over the entire mess, swung on a tripod over a roaring fire and brought to a boil. There, it would simmer for hours.

Fish were plentiful year-round, but J. Carothers, who advertised himself as restaurateur, a dealer in ice and German carp, was the proprietor of the Buchanan German Carp Ponds. Turtle meat was big and was often made into soup or cut into chunks and fried.

Other meals might have included fried squirrel, stewed onions and potatoes cooked in butter.

Pine Lake Inn on Pine Lake in LaPorte. The lake is well stocked with a variety of fish, including large-mouthed bass, bluegills, sunfish, perches and blue catfish. For entertainment, there was dancing at the pavilions on the Pine Lake Assembly Grounds and on steamboats. *LaPorte County Historical Society Museum.*

Diarists recalled Johnny cakes with fresh butter and molasses, fresh vegetables grown in the gardens next to the taverns and peach, strawberry or apricot or preserves to spread on bread.

As one might expect, meat dominated—turkey, venison, beef mutton and pork, wild duck, chicken, goose, passenger pigeon (until they became extinct), rabbit and turtle. A meal might also consist of skunk, beaver, bear (a very greasy meat) or racoon (the latter said to be one of Abraham Lincoln's favorite meals), jerked or dried beef, veal, bacon and ham. The latter two would be made by the innkeepers, who would hang them to dry and smoke them over a low fire.

Milk and buttermilk were generally available because innkeepers kept cows, but real coffee was hard to come by. Instead, people drank what was called coffee, but the drink was really made from roasted grains. English tea was also hard to get and was expensive, so tea was made from roots and plants like mint and sassafras. Pies and puddings were plentiful when fruit was in season, and cordials would also be made from fruit.

Until the 1850s, only the best of hotels had bathrooms, so guests made do with a jug of water, a bowl and a towel (which others had probably used as well) and a chamber pot as a substitute for a toilet. These chamber pots might be placed in a shared room or outside. Either way, they were for everyone to use.

A typical breakfast, made by the landlady, at a small tavern might have consisted of oiled eggs, bread and tea and cost about twenty-five cents.

A typical tavern meal could include salt pork boiled with turnip tops, a warm salad dressed with vinegar and frying pan fat. At one place, there was salted mutton that was, as one guest described it, "seasoned with dirt." One traveler recalled being served a bowl of milk and a piece of bread. The milk was sweet, but the bread dry and stale, and when he placed it in the bowl, red bugs rose "kicking most lustily to the surface, where they were immediately skimmed off and most barbarously committed to the flames."

Fingers were used in place of forks, and guests were expected to bring their own knives. The more particular guests probably brought their own forks as well. Because water wasn't safe to drink, people indulged in alcohol and, as a result, were slightly soused, having started off with ale in the morning and continued to the harder stuff as the day went on.

It didn't take much to establish a drinking place. In 1833, a Canadian named Ruleaux built a log house in Bainbridge Township and stocked it with a few bottles of whisky and called it a tavern.

The first food truck? Celebrating fruit packets during a celebration in Benton Harbor in 1875. *St. Joseph Public Library.*

The Washington House in South Bend opened in 1837 and was considered a fine hotel for such a small community. That was the same year the Traveler's Rest opened as well.

Martin Dodge owned the Colfax House in Benton Harbor. It isn't known if Dodge was related to Daniel. It's also unknown whether he buried his wife in the backyard.

Henry and Margaret Diehl opened the Franklin House in South Bend. Mr. Diehl, a baker by trade, was known for his delicious gingerbread, described as dark brown from his use of molasses from New Orleans. He also made a type of root beer. Both were said to be popular with customers, but his greatest attraction, according to David Rohrer Leeper's *Early Inns and Taverns of South Bend*, was a musical clock in which musicians appeared as the music played. Such was the need for entertainment back then.

Pierce's Tavern in Goshen was a stop on the coach road between Detroit, Fort Wayne and Chicago. It was a rudimentary place. Eli Penwell also had a

The Ace Lunch Room, under the management of Lyn Schilla and Howard Tait, opened at 110 Water Street in Benton Harbor on February 15, 1945, with a menu featuring Coney Island hot dogs, vegetables, chili, hamburgers, homemade baked beans and potato salad. *Benton Harbor Public Library.*

A steamer landing at Somerleyton on the St. Joseph River. *Benton Harbor Public Library.*

tavern where coaches exchanged horses. When the stage came, so came those who lived nearby, eager to hear the local news.

Clark Pennell and his father ran the Buckhorn Tavern, another structure built of logs, on the Saint Joseph Road. As for the name? A pair of buck's horns were hung over the tavern shed by Wm. H. Tryon, who was a noted deer hunter. In a time when many couldn't read and addresses were rudimentary, the horns let people know they were in the right place.

William Parkinson's Stagecoach Line operated in La Porte County from the 1840s to the 1870s. Described as a tall man who wore a silk hat—a rather dashing look for someone who rode high on a stagecoach in the rain and snow—he charged passengers $1.25 to ride between La Porte and Valparaiso and $0.75 for the trip from Westville to Captain Eli's house in LaPorte (it would later be replaced by the much posher Teegarden Hotel), which took two hours. The trip between LaPorte to Westville—a distance of about twelve miles, or about sixteen minutes by car today—took two hours (and that is if everything went smoothly, which we know it often didn't).

In 1862, at a Fourth of July celebration in Westville, Parkinson, wearing a long duster, set off some fireworks. Unfortunately, the entire batch of fireworks burst into flames, and Parkinson, panicking after seeing his duster on fire, didn't drop and roll; instead, he ran, fanning the flames. After the fire was extinguished, he was credited with being the first long-tailed meteor ever sighted in La Porte County—pioneer humor, probably aided by some ghastly tasting whiskey.

One traveler described a tavern where there were rows of glass decanters, each labeled with well-known brands of whiskey and gin, but despite the fancy names it all came from common barrels that cost the owner about twenty cents a gallon.

One imagines these were dark, dark places with few if any windows and homemade booze that probably wasn't meant to be savored but rather consumed as quickly as possible and sure to cause severe hangovers the next morning.

Taverns were more than just places to drink. People (or at least men) congregated so they served as social centers as well and lawyers used them as their offices, and some taverns were the sites of the state legislative meetings and even courtrooms.

Besides dirt, in the summer flies were a serious issue, particularly at inns where there was a manure pile by the door. Sometimes, there were peacock feathers available to swat them away. Bedsheets were often used as tablecloths and vice versa without being washed in between.

The walkway leading from the piers to the Whitcomb and Lakeview Hotels. *St. Joseph Public Library*.

Early days for Tabor Resort with a notation that Ma Tabor is standing in the front yard. The resort was located nine miles southeast of Benton Harbor. *St. Joseph Public Library*.

The Lakeview and Whitcomb Hotels, in the early 1900s, were perched above the St. Joseph River, overlooking Lake Michigan. The Whitcomb is still standing. *St. Joseph Public Library.*

Some men spoke of dirty taverns, dirty meals and dirty women—though one can't imagine the men were any cleaner.

Whiskey was a universal alcoholic beverage in the Midwest, as it was cheap. Fermented fruit drinks, like hard cider and blackberry brandy, were common as well. Cherry bounce was another popular drink, and sherry cobblers were made from mixing a dozen eggs, a pound of sugar, a little milk and a lot of whiskey. It was then cooked and served communally, with participants using spoons or whatever they had to eat it up.

2
EARLY TIMES

As settlements grew, hotels became more common. Built in 1831, the Mansion House was the first hotel built in Saint Joseph and stood on the corner of State and Broad Streets. The name Mansion House was an insult, because the structure was built of logs, and it was not a mansion—nor was it much of a house. But its panoramic view of the water was stunning. And for business purposes, it was just right; its location made it an overnight stop for the Detroit to Chicago stage. It also served as a post office where people could get their mail.

It also served another purpose. The first marriage in what was then called Newberryport took place there when Captain Calvin Bartlett married Pamela Ives. A year later (for those keeping count, and back then they did), Amos Bartlett was born, becoming the first white child born in what would become Saint Joseph.

Calvin Lilly's Hotel in South Bend in 1831 was said to provide the choicest liquors around.

In 1834, the Michigan House was built below the bluff and catered mainly to those who were traveling along the Saint Joseph River. And there was nothing genteel about those who plied their trade on the river and those who served them. The classic working women met working men, and money was exchanged for favors. According to the March 21, 1903 edition of the *St. Joseph Saturday Herald*, when Mayor Nelson Rice took office, St. Joseph had at least seven brothels. Besides that, many of the saloons were known to have slot machines, plus there were gambling establishments scattered around the

Edgewood Court Cabin and Restaurant on Lakeshore Drive, four miles south of St. Joseph, Michigan, and ninety-five miles from Chicago on US 12. It has sixteen modern cabins, running water, restaurant, shuffleboard, cool and shady beach privileges, spacious grounds and private shower. *Benton Harbor Public Library.*

city. Rice is credited with closing a lot of the houses of prostitution, probably to the chagrin of many who frequented such places, and the women who unfortunately had to make their living doing so.

One observer at the time described the river and its taverns as a scene of much hilarity from frolicking, as well as the setting of many a terrible fight.

Daniel Earl took out a license to open Earl's Tavern in what became known as Lakeville, a town south of South Bend.

To the local papers, the most famous of the old hotels in Saint Joseph was the three-story Perkins House. Built in 1840, it stood on the corner of State and Ship Streets. It had both a balcony and a real parlor, where, according to a description, guests were expected to sit stiffly on horsehair chairs.

B.C. Hoyt erected the White House in 1867 and it, too, became one of the city's premiere hotels. When the Walker family took over, the name changed to the Lakeview Hotel and remained open until 1924.

Torn down in 1866, the Mansion House was replaced by the Saint Charles Hotel, which was built two years later. The site would ultimately become the location of the Whitcomb Hotel, which still stands today.

The Whitcomb was considered the finest hotel in the area, attracting a clientele of wealthy summer tourists who expected the luxury and magnificence of great city hotels. They were delighted to experience the magnificence the Whitcomb offered.

An aerial view of the river and harbor in St. Joseph and Benton Harbor. *The Tichnor Brothers Collection, Boston Public Library.*

There's no other identification for this restaurant on East Main Street in Benton Harbor, but there is a building with a similar style still standing in the city's historic arts district. In the photograph, dated January 31, 1909, there appears to have been a serious snowstorm. *Benton Harbor Public Library.*

In 1850, Gilson Osgood bought a tavern owned by Moses Sargent on the corner of Saint Joseph and Paw Paw Streets in Coloma and turned it into a fine hotel. He also operated a livery stable, so while the passengers were dining or spending the night, the horses could rest or be switched out. Miss Helen Becker was the hotel's cook.

Enlistees in the Civil War marched to the Osgood Hotel, where they took the stage to Saint Joseph to join other enlistees. Let's hope they got to enjoy some of Miss Becker's cooking.

"The first 'restaurant' in what is now Dowagiac was the tavern/inn at McOmber's stagecoach stop at North Front and Prairie Ronde Streets," wrote Steve Arseneau, the director of the Dowagiac Area History Museum. "After the railroad's arrival in 1848, hotels opened with taverns and restaurants attached. Early inns included the American House and the Dowagiac House. Nicholas Bock's American House even fed the kids who arrived on the first orphan train in 1853. Few residents opened full-time restaurants in the city's early history."

People did some serious drinking back then. Between 1860 to 1881, Dowagiac had twelve saloons and was known as "the worst whiskey hole." It's really a lovely small town now.

JACOB WAGNER RESTAURANT AND Saloon opened in 1867 in South Bend. Four years later, it was one of the first in the city to feature fresh oysters (they arrived by train) on its menu.

The *Saint Joseph City Directory* from 1870 states that the restaurants, hotels and taverns included the National Hotel on Main Street, Peter Weckler's Saloon at 59 Main Street, Krieger Billiards and Saloon at 5 Ship Street (owned by Charles Krieger) and Melsheimer's Saloon at 9 State Street.

In 1881, the *South Bend Tribune* reported that there were six restaurants open for business in the city proper, including those owned by Mrs. Gould Johnson, D.W. Russ, James Patten, L. Nickel Jr. and Co., A.F. Vanderhoof, and Hyatt and DeMarcellonni. The newspaper pondered why there were so many restaurants, since the city had numerous boardinghouses where residents could take their meals.

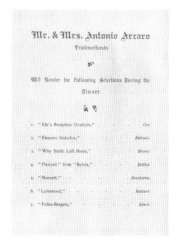

A special musical performance at a dinner at the Oliver. *The History Museum.*

Originally known as the Jewell Hotel when it was built in 1893, the hotel's name was changed to Hotel Vreeland and was known as one of the most luxurious hotels in Northern Indiana with an elevator, tile floors, steam heat and electric lights. By 1898, the demand for rooms was such that the hotel was expanded. *LaPorte County Historical Society*.

The first Oliver House opened in South Bend on the evening of July 14, 1879, and it closed almost nineteen years later to make way for the new and much more elegant Oliver House. The six-story hotel cost $600,000 to build and was beyond elegant. It was described as "The Best and Most Magnificent Hotel in Indiana, one of the finest in the United States, and the Best in Any City of 40,000 Inhabitants in the World."

Ed Jamott, the owner of a tavern that bore his name, advertised bock beer on draught in the late 1890s.

The Corn Exchange in South Bend was presided over by Billy Mason, who purchased an interest in the place in 1888.

With so many saloons in the area—many of which weren't licensed originally—the Anti-Saloon League soon gained traction there. By the early 1900s, long before Prohibition was enacted, hotels, restaurants and taverns were being shut down. According to the May 8, 1915 edition of the *Saint Joseph Saturday Herald*, hundreds turned out to celebrate the closing of the saloons the night before they were shut down.

Though one can't expect to get an ice cream cone, lunch or soda at Walgreen's or CVS today, back in the late 1800s and well into the mid-1950s, dime stores and drugstores had lunch counters, soda fountains and ornate luncheon areas.

THE
SODA ROOM

Delicious Chocolate
Sodas and numerous
Fountain Specialties
to refresh you in the
delightful surroundings
of our Soda Room.

Gillespie's Drug Store
Saint Joseph
Michigan

The soda room at Gillespie's Drugstore in downtown St. Joseph, circa the 1920s. *St. Joseph Public Library*.

Scott's Pharmacy was the local stop for the Greyhound bus route that offered special round-trip rates to Chicago from Kalamazoo, Grand Rapids, Muskegon and all intervening points, according to an advertisement in the June 18, 1926 edition of the *Coloma Courier*. *Benton Harbor Public Library.*

The St. Joseph Walkway from the piers up the bluff to the hotels. *St. Joseph Public Library.*

Several soft drinks took the place of alcohol at places like the Lake View Buffet, John Kibler and Son, Frank Ludwig and Daniel Muth. Others, such as the Hotel Whitcomb and buffets owned by John Morlock, Hassle and Zordell and Paul Bodjack, announced they would close their doors. Shutting down saloons had a negative financial impact on many people, forcing long-established businesses to close their doors. As examples, according to the papers, John Kibler had been engaged in the business since 1876, and Albert Ankli had been dispensing drinks for twenty-three years.

Patrons helped the owners clear out their stock, and many saloons were dry by 11:00 p.m. The lights were turned out as the crowd swarmed into the dark streets.

Bar owners hoped that without any liquor sales being allowed at all, people would rebel and vote to open the saloons again.

Professor George Dierstein, the leader of the Saint Joseph City Band, made the rounds to all the saloons after closing time that Friday night and sounded "Taps."

The next day, bar owner Frank Ludwig was serving buttermilk and pop with his lunches. Schuyler Unruh and Hendrick and Haines also served soft drinks in their places in Benton Harbor. One does wonder what they might have been serving under the counter, so to speak.

They may have been going out of business, but they were doing it in style.

3
ON THE WATER

THE LAKES

Starting in the late 1800s, steamships plied the waters between Chicago and Saint Joseph, disembarking passengers who could ride, for fifty cents, the moving walkway up the hill to the town and then stay in one of the large wooden resorts, like the Saint Joseph Hotel and the Lakeview, or catch an interurban and then a trolley to the many resorts lining the shores of Paw Paw Lake.

With the advent of highways, motorists could travel to the seven Sister Lakes near Dowagiac or travel along the eastern shore of Lake Michigan from Michigan City to Saint Joseph and then to Benton Harbor.

Across the Indiana border going into Michigan, there were resorts in the Lake Michigan beachfront communities, like the Gordon Beach Inn, the Inn at Union Pier, the Lakeside Inn and, for Lithuanians, Ginatara's. The first three are still in business.

Bit of Swiss Bakery opened in 1967. But before that, baker Hans Kottman worked at the Whitcomb Hotel. When that business closed, Emil Tosi bought the equipment and renovated a cabin next to his restaurant. Both Tosi's and Bit of Swiss, which has expanded quite a bit since those cabin days and was named the best bakery in the country by a trade magazine several years ago, are still in business.

Rick Rasmussen, the author of several books, including *Sister Lakes* (Arcadia Publishing, 2007), tells the story of the lakes through postcards

The Chicago Hotel at Forest Beach on Paw Paw Lake in 1910. Two years earlier, a 130-foot-long pier was built into the lake to accommodate gasoline launches and steamboats. The old pier remained for rowboats and other launches, according to the June 5, 1908 *Watervliet Record*. *North Berrien History Museum*.

The Coloma trolley that took passengers to the resorts on Paw Paw Lake. *North Berrien Historical Museum*.

Bit of Swiss, an award-winning bakery, opened in 1967 and is next to Tosi's Restaurant in Stevensville, Michigan. *Jane Simon Ammeson.*

A 1929 postcard of the Fairview Hotel in Michigan City. The ladies dressed in white were visiting the annual chautauqua, which lasted between five and seven days. There were also chautauquas in South Bend and Mishawaka, and important people spoke at the one in South Bend, including Teddy Roosevelt in 1915 and Willian Jennings Bryan two years after that. *La Porte County Historical Society.*

Elaborate soda fountains, like the one at Scott's Pharmacy in Coloma, were extremely popular. *Benton Harbor Public Library*.

dating from the late 1800s to the mid-1900s, is also an amateur historian who grew up in the Sister Lakes area.

The Rasmussen roots go back more than a century. The family celebrated their centennial there almost two decades ago.

Wanting to share and preserve that history, Rasmussen takes us back to a time when large hotels dotted the shorelines of the Sister Lakes, a string of inland lakes tucked into the rolling hills of Southwest Michigan.

At the Sandy Beach Resort on Dewey Lake in Dowagiac, Michigan, crisp white tablecloths covered seemingly endless rows of tables that were able to seat four hundred people at a time. Some were just as fancy as the dining rooms in the bigger cities, like LaPorte, Michigan City, Benton Harbor and even Chicago. "Most of the resorts had American plans where wonderful meals were included," Rasmussen told me when I interviewed him a few years ago.

By the 1920s, according to Rasmussen, Sandy Beach was such a large operation that its owner, F.E. Tarrant, contracted with a company in Chicago to run brightly painted buses from the city to Dewey Lake on a scheduled basis.

A steamer landing at Somerleyton on the St. Joseph River. *Benton Harbor Public Library.*

"Your home is our only competitor" reads the back of the postcard from the Rose Inn Family Style and Rose Inn Cottages Resort, which was owned by Mr. and Mrs. L.R. McCrea and located on Paw Paw Lake. Private parties and banquets are "our specialty." *Jane Simon Ammeson.*

Shady Shores Resort on Dewey Lake in Dowagiac, Michigan. Besides Dewey, the seven lakes comprising Sister Lakes are Big Crooked Lake, Little Crooked Lake, Cable Lake, Magician Lake and Round Lake. *The Tichnor Brothers Collection, Boston Public Library.*

Besides Sandy Beach, Dewey Lake was also home to Shady Shores Resort, Dehnhardt Lodge and Garrett's Farm Home Resort. Rasmussen describes the latter as an example of an area farm that became a summer resort. "If you want to really enjoy your vacation at a small cost and if you want to live the simple life on a 140-acre farm, Garrett's Farm offers a rolled lawn for tennis, baseball diamond, croquet and games," reads a passage from a 1915 brochure that was quoted in Rasmussen's book. Vacationers could also hunt, fish, swim and go boating.

"Every day there was all the fresh fruit, eggs, and milk one could eat and drink," wrote Rasmussen. "The resort could hold up to 40 people at a time. The cost for food and lodging was $7 per week. No children were allowed during the month of August."

Hunters looked for not only game such as deer, rabbit and squirrel, but they also hunted frogs—frog legs were menu favorites back then. And that, unfortunately, led to tragedy on June 6, 1938, when three young men drowned while hunting bullfrogs. The victims were Earl Wiest Jr., the son of the proprietor of Wiest's Resort at Indian Lake; Frank Clark of Dowagiac; and Frank Bratek of Chicago, who had been spending a ten-day holiday at the lake. No one witnessed the accident, but at 11:30 a.m. on Sunday, their rowboat, containing only a broken oar and the rifle they would have used to shoot frogs, drifted to the shore near Wiest's Resort. By 7:30 p.m., the bodies were discovered in about 12 feet of water 150 feet from shore. It was surmised that Bratek, who couldn't swim, fell into the water and the other two attempted to save him. Ironically, Bratek had been rescued just a week earlier by Clark and another man from Dowagiac. Sadly, Wiest's mother had drowned in Indian Lake five years earlier.

But these were tragic and devastating exceptions. For the most part, during the summer season, the resorts were filled with the sounds of laughter, fun and music. When Earl Wiest celebrated the opening of the Garret Club, a new dining and nightclub at his resort in 1935, he had an all-star lineup of entertainers, including Rex Gallion, a classic musician who played mandolin, banjo, accordion and guitar.

"So much has changed," Rasmussen told me when we spoke. It was while doing research on Paw Paw Lake that Rasmussen started collecting postcards from the lake and had collected, when we talked, 920. He values them so much that he keeps them in a safe deposit box. "You think you've got them all, and then there's another one," he said. He became so enamored of his

The Hotel Whitcomb piped nearby sulfur spring water into hotel baths. Sulfur water has a distinct odor—some compare it to spoiled eggs—and the scent sometimes lingered in the air. *Benton Harbor Public Library.*

PICNIC TABLES AT SILVER BEACH PARK, ST. JOSEPH, MICH.   D-275

The picnic area at Silver Beach in St. Joseph. The boardwalk was lined with food vendors, including Rosie's, which is now open during the Berrien County Youth Fair each August. *St. Joseph Public Library.*

hobby that he joined the Southwest Michigan Post Card Club, where he met a fellow collector, Floyd Jerdon, who owned a real estate business in Dowagiac with his son. "With his son, he's third generation," said Rasmussen. "And his family is involved in local history. Years ago, he started collecting post cards, and now he's got a couple thousand of the Sister Lakes area, which are in a vault at the bank."

Arcadia had wanted Rasmussen to write a book about Sister Lakes.

"Jerdon had the postcards to put it together, but he had a business to run," he said. "So, I did the research. I spent the whole winter talking to people, and in working with local history, one person leads to another."

Rasmussen was also able to call on the research that Jerdon's realty company had done to get information on plats and other developments. "They had data which no one else had," he said. "So much of that is gone now."

"Technically," Rasmussen writes in his book's introduction, "the two lakes called Sister Lakes are Round and Crooked."

"By 1877, there were enough people in the region for the United States government to open a post office," he wrote. "Since it was located between the two lakes, it was named Sister Lakes." But geographically, Rasmussen's

A 1905 photograph of the Carmody Brothers Drugstore and soda fountain in Watervliet. *North Berrien Historical Museum.*

Crooked Lake, one of the Sister Lakes in Dowagiac, Michigan. *The Tichnor Brothers Collection, Boston Public Library.*

books include nine other lakes that are within a six-mile radius and are considered part of the Sister Lakes area: Magician, which has three islands (Maple, Scouts and Hemlock); Indian; Dewey; Little Crooked; Cable; Keeler; Pipestone; Priest; and Brush.

Other places say there are seven but I'm going with Rasmussen on this.

The eleven lakes, Rasmussen said, are in the corner of three counties, Cass, Berrien and Van Buren, and three townships, Bainbridge, Keeler and Silver Creek. "Each has its own personality and lifestyle," he said.

The lakes started attracting vacationers in the 1880s as people began to earn enough money to take vacations, and the Sister Lakes became the perfect vacation spot. Not far from Chicago and even closer to South Bend, there was sun, water, great food, dance pavilions, boating, steamships, canoeing, campfires and all sorts of fun. Farms became resorts, sometimes enticing people with the opportunity to pick fruit and do other chores. Lake frontage turned into valuable lots for cottages.

The vintage photographs in Rasmussen's book recall an era before television, computers and video games. Men wore hats to sit on the front porch of old wood lodges. Women vacationed in skirts that dusted the ground and stiffly starched white shirts with high necks, bonnets and straw hats and bathing suits that reached below the knee. Boys wore suits with short pants and large white collars. Cars were Model Ts. At Wiest's Resort on Edgewater

Ernie Wiest's Resort on Indian Lake in Dowagiac. *The Tichnor Brothers Collection, Boston Public Library.*

WHIP POOR WILL HOTEL - LITTLE PAW PAW LAKE, MICH.

Will-O-Paw was a resort on Paw Paw Lake. *North Berrien Historical Museum.*

Beach on Indian Lake, there was a three-story diving apparatus that would never pass today's safety regulations. The same goes for the Safe-T Rail, a three-story wooden slide at Wiest's Resort. Rasmussen described it thus: "One or two people would carry a slide with wheels to the top, sit down, push themselves off and end up propelled into the water."

During the 1930s, the oddly named Smallbones Resort on Sister Lake hosted a yearly daylong event for members of the Saint Joseph Lodge of Elks with a steak and fried chicken meal served at noon and baseball, fishing and horseshoes for entertainment.

The bill of fare at the Ellinee Village Inn in 1932 featured chicken, steak or fish dinners for one dollar. Frog legs would cost you an extra twenty-five cents. Dinner consisted of shrimp cocktail, a fruit bowl, a salad, a consommé and a choice of vegetables and French fries, dessert and either beer or coffee.

This early resort development spurred additional development of resort and hotel activities. Places to stay included the Manhattan Hotel, Edgewater, Birds Nest Hotel, Never Mind Hotel, Shauls' Villa, Wiest's Resort, Ridenour Farm and Resort and Tice landing. These early resorts were frequently added on to, becoming larger and larger with the continuing influx of tourists.

The entrance to the Ellinee, a longtime popular resort on Paw Paw Lake. *St. Joseph Public Library.*

The Edgewater on Indian Lake in Dowagiac, Michigan. Until 1915, the resorts on Indian Lake were known for their excellent fish dinners, but a new law enacted that year stopped the commercial sale of privately caught fish, and according to the Indian Lake Improvement Association, serving fish dinners was considered selling fish. *Northern Berrien Historical Museum.*

Eden Springs Park Food Cart. *St. Joseph Public Library.*

To get tourists to their destinations, vessels such as the steamer *Margaret* and the *Fenetta L*, a craft built in 1901 that operated out of Tuttle's Landing on Indian Lake, transported passengers to the growing number of resorts lining the lake. Originally a steamer, it acquired a Studebaker engine in 1928. After years of service, the *Fenetta L* was scuttled off Tuttle's Landing, which became Indian Beach in 1914 and is now the Indian Lake Yacht Club. It's said that at times, ice fishers have been able to spot the hull of the boat. It was one of many boats that transported guests. Looking now at the overcrowding and heavy clothing that people wore, it makes one wonder if there were any safety regulations.

While researching the book, Rasmussen discovered more families like his, who have been in the area for generations. "Floyd is a classic example," he said. "His family came here in the 1940s from the Dust Bowl area and got a farm. But they almost lost it. The only reason they were able to save it is because his mother raised chickens and sold the eggs to tourists on Indian Lake."

One of my favorite vintage photographs from the area shows the speedboat *King Tut* on Indian Lake in 1929. Earl Wiest Jr. and Ralph Tice, the owners of Tice's Beach at the north end of Indian Lake, were business

Forest Hall on Diamond Lake. *North Berrien Historical Museum.*

rivals, and that spilled over into other areas, including whose boat was the fastest. Tice owned *King Tut*, the fastest boat on the lake, and showed off its speed by racing it in front of Wiest's Resort.

The resorts weren't just a man's world. There were women who took advantage of the tourism boom and ran their own hotels and inns. The family of Jane Ethel Granzow Miles owned the Manley Resort. It started simply enough, according to the history Miles wrote about her family, when a stranger knocked on her grandmother's door in 1905 looking for a quiet spot to stay and liked the country feel of their property with its fruit trees. Oh, and he wanted a good homecooked meal. Things obviously were different back then, but grandma said yes. And seeing a golden opportunity, within two years, an advertisement for the Manley House read "boarding house on the Joseph River Bluff, one mile from town, large grounds, good house everything pleasant, accommodations for $1.25 per day, $7.00 to $8.00 per week. Meet boats or trains on request."

The house, which still stands and is a private residence, overlooks the St. Joseph River and is on Langley Avenue.

Before long, according to Gina J. Grillo in her article in the *Northwest Indiana Times* titled "Resorting Women: Victorian Era Proprietors & Pastimes," which ran on April 7, 2013, other women owners included Mrs. C.S. Jenks, the proprietor of Pleasant View Farm; Mrs. A.W. Rapelje, the proprietor of the Maplewood Hotel; and Mrs. Spink, the proprietor of the Spring Bluff Resort. Not listed was Mrs. Cummings, who, along with her husband, ran the first lodging house for travelers in New Buffalo. Mrs. Mary DeField ran the DeField House in Berrien Springs, and Mrs. Mary Morrison was the proprietor of a hotel in Stevensville. Jane M. Hooper owned an inn in Decatur.

The Woodward House on Paw Paw Lake was operated by Mrs. O.W. Woodward, whose place was described in an issue of the *Resorter* as "so favorably known and the credit is due to Mrs. O.W. Woodward, for her place is 'Just Like Home.'"

Then there was Lydia Wilkinson, nicknamed the "Renaissance Woman of Lakeside," who, at the beginning of the twentieth century, owned, with her husband, the Pine Bluff Hotel Resort in Lakeside, Michigan. According to Grillo, Lydia, along with her neighbor Maud Perham, saw a need and began the area's first taxi service for tourists, meeting Chicago visitors in Lakeside at the railroad station in their Model Ts and offering transport to area lodgings. Mrs. Wilkinson's contributions to resort life in Lakeside were abundant. She hosted open-air teas and hikes along Lake Michigan's shoreline.

Tucked away on the dirt roads leading through Grand Mere, a wooded area with three lakes that backs up to the dunes on Lake Michigan, the Grand Mere Inn was a place for visitors to get away from city life and enjoy hiking and foraging. The name Grand Mere Inn was appropriated by the Racine family, who founded the Grand Mere Inn on Red Arrow Highway in Stevensville. The restaurant overlooks the dunes and the lake. Rates were $15 and up. Home-cooked meals used ingredients as much as possible that were fresh from the farm and gardens. In 1969, people could also stop by for their "little country dinners" that cost $1.25.

Social dancing was much more popular than it is now. It wasn't just for the young but was enjoyed by all. Both the Sister Lakes and Paw Paw Lake had plenty of places to dance, including on the piers that jutted into the water. At the Ramona, a popular Sister Lakes dance hall, dances were held every night, with Jack Wedell, the boy with the million dollar voice, and his new and greater orchestra providing the music.

In 1938, Shadowland Ballroom at Silver Beach featured dancing every evening with Jack Jill & his Orchestra and advertised "Singing and Dancing Galore."

You could dance nightly (except on Mondays) at the Woodward Pier on Paw Lake to music by Buddy Walker and his Columbia Broadcasting Orchestra. The Woodward Pavilion was one of several and included the Edgewater Pavilion where Ray Kroc, who would go on to found

You could dance nightly (except on Mondays) at the Woodward Pier on Paw Paw Lake to music by Buddy Walker and his Columbia Broadcasting Orchestra. *Northern Berrien Historical Museum.*

McDonald's, played piano in 1919. According to Rick Rasmussen, Kroc met his first wife, Ethel Flemming, at the Edgewater. Her parents were the owners of the May-Bell Hotel at Lakewood Point. Kroc and the band played on one of the boats that plied the waters along the shoreline while another person stood on the bow, shouting out, "Dance tonight at the Edgewater! Don't miss out on the fun!"

Kay Kyser and his Orchestra performed at the Crystal Palace on Paw Paw Lake on Wednesday, July 3. Admission cost ninety cents in advance and one dollar at the door. The Crystal Palace also offered dancing every evening until Labor Day, with music by Thurman Teague's Orchestra, NBC artists. Admission was free.

If all that dancing made you hungry, Ed's Café, located five hundred feet east of Crystal Palace on Paw Paw Lake, advertised a complete fried chicken dinner for fifty cents, along with steak, barbecue sandwiches and beer. And not to worry about the time. It was open at all hours.

The Pit Barbecue Shop, at 214 State Street, was owned by Mr. and Mrs. L.L. Brown and specialized in barbecues turned on spits over a charcoal blaze in an open brick pit at the rear of the shop. The building was redecorated and modernized in rose, silver and blue, with booths and tables in natural pine. Counter seats were yellow leather.

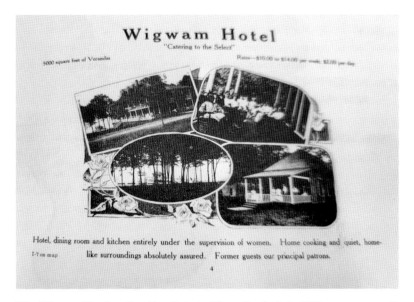

The Wigwam Hotel on Paw Paw Lake in Watervliet, built in 1898, was open until 1963. It was then sold and turned into a private residence before both the hotel building and annex burned down in 2010. *North Berrien Historical Museum.*

You could get a complete fried chicken dinner for fifty cents along with steak, barbecue sandwiches and beer at Ed's Café, located five hundred feet east of Crystal Palace on Paw Paw Lake at all hours. *North Berrien Historical Museum.*

Brown and Brownie American Beer Gardens at 192 Colfax Avenue in Benton Harbor featured dancing every night, with floor shows and Don's Music Makers providing an evening of pleasure. "Good Food—Good Beer—Good Time" and no minimum or cover charge.

"Spend a Day at The Koffee Shoppe." Located eight miles north of Benton Harbor on U.S. 31, there was dancing on Wednesday and Saturday evenings, a bathing beach, picnic grounds, chicken and steak dinners, delicious sandwiches and "hamburgs" (there was no "er" in the advertisement). The cost of cabins started at one dollar a day, and modern housekeeping cottages went for eighteen dollars a week.

Ernie Erickson, an artist and engraver from Chicago, moved to Coloma in 1908 and grew his souvenir stand into the fabulous Ellinee, with its artist colony, five-foot tower, gable, dance floor and bowling alley, as well as a one-hundred-foot pier jutting into the lake.

Boats, trolleys and trains took people to all-inclusive resorts—or the 1900s version of them—where all they needed for fun and a comfy stay was provided. Some didn't make it as far north as Saint Joseph and instead enjoyed the large resorts in Michigan City, such as the Golfmore, a magnificent place on Lake Michigan.

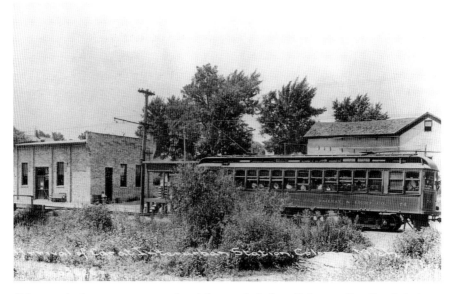

Coloma train depot, a stop on a railroad that was built from Coloma to Paw Paw Lake in 1896 to provide access to the lake resorts. Train records show forty thousand people traveled to the lake each summer. *North Berrien Historical Museum.*

Golfmore Hotel, located just across the state line in Michiana Shores, Indiana, opened in 1921. With 175 rooms, the Golfmore could accommodate some five hundred guests and also had 250 public rooms for guests to enjoy. In winter, the Golfmore held ski jumping events. If that sounds odd now, know it wasn't back then. There was skiing in Miller Beach and Ogden Dunes, both farther west along the lakeshore. In the 1930s, Charles S. Knapp was the hotel proprietor. *LaPorte County Historical Society.*

Bluffside Pavilion on the Bluffside Beach on Pine Lake in LaPorte, Indiana. *LaPorte County Historical Society.*

There was golfing for those staying at the many resorts on Pine Lake at the La Porte Country Club. *LaPorte County Historical Society Museum.*

In 1921, it was announced that of the forty cottages at the Pine Lake Inn, thirty-eight had already been rented out before the season began, mostly to Chicagoans. Many of the resorts held clam bakes, fish fries and corn roasts, as well as other types of entertainment in those pre-television and cellphone days. *LaPorte County Historical Society Museum.*

The Golfmore wasn't just for summer fun. It also had an adjacent ski ramp that attracted even the University of Wisconsin ski team and a twenty-seven-hole golf course. Built in the early 1920s, the resort was busted several times for selling booze during Prohibition and offering gambling as one of its amenities.

Besides the Golfmore, Michigan City had other fancy hotels, such as the Fairview and the Sheridan.

Chautauquas were popular in the late 1800s and early 1900s, attracting thousands of people. According to the LaPorte County Historical Society's website, these events were called "traveling cyclopedias…with people coming from all over to [enjoy] education, inspiration, and recreation." The summer educational center, on the northern border of Pine Lake, seated 1,800 people who came to listen to the speakers.

SOUNDING VERY MODERN AND New Age, "the location on Pine Lake was designed to take advantage of the assembly of numerous persons with a 'oneness of purpose.'"

It was believed that the "close proximity of human beings renders them keenly susceptible to the mental and emotional influence of gifted speakers." Cottages and hotels on Pine Lake provided places for people to stay, as the chautauqua grounds were located on the northern edge of the water.

Most resorts at the time were family owned.

Vytas Ambutas grew up on the Pottawatomie Resort that his parents owned. It comprised 120 acres of Lake Michigan frontage in Coloma and offered vacations according to the American plan. Sprawling resorts like these were popular until the 1960s and '70s, when things began to change. Another special sprawling place was Tabor Farm on the Saint Joseph River. Families would return year after year to these self-contained resorts with their large dining halls, game rooms, tennis courts, swimming pools and lots of other activities to keep families busy. Of course, the game room didn't feature such video games as *Pac-Man*; rather, it had pinball machines. It also had a cocktail lounge called the Driftwood, and for a while, it had a summer theater and a cook who whipped up fried chicken, meat loaf, pork chops, mashed potatoes, peas and fried perch.

But running a large resort isn't easy. "Try and find someone who can fix a cable car motor for the cable car that takes people down to the beach," Ambutas said.

The 160-acre Tabor Farm, which opened in 1891 or 1893, depending on the source, and was located on the St. Joseph River in Sodus, was considered one of the first modern resorts in Southwest Michigan. *The Tichnor Brothers Collection, Boston Public Library.*

But in this line of work, you do meet interesting people and learn some skills. "I used to help Wilbur Fikes, who was an electrician," recalls Ambutas. "He could tell whether a socket was live by sticking a screwdriver in it." Maybe that isn't a good skill to learn.

There were also resorts along the Saint Joseph River as it wound its way southeast from Lake Michigan. Tabor Hill was one of them.

Football fans could take the South Shore, now the only remaining interurban in the United States, to Notre Dame football games.

Travelers could stay at motels, where they could also grab a bite to eat and gas up as well. Many of the little ma-and-pa type motels offered home-cooked meals and were popular with locals.

As the motel era progressed, chains, such as Howard Johnson's, began taking over. Interestingly, famed French chef Jacques Pépin worked at a Howard Johnson's as a line chef.

Between 1920 and 1930, the number of automobiles in America rose from eight million to twenty-three million, and along with this increase came thousands of barbeque shacks, ice cream stands and diners. These restaurants and stands catered to motorists, travelers and tourists, like the Howard Johnson's Ice Cream Stands that popped up in Boston in the mid-1920s, later evolving into the hotel and restaurant chain.

"Across the Lake," Notre Dame,
Notre Dame, Indiana

Notre Dame's campus attracts hundreds of thousands of visitors each year for many reasons—its football games, two lakes, the Grotto of Our Lady of Lourdes, its beauty and its historic buildings and art. There are guided tours available year-round. *The Tichnor Brothers Collection, Boston Public Library.*

GINGHAM INN . . . U. S. Hwy. 20 . . . 4 Miles West of Michigan City, Ind.

Gingham Inn was located on U.S. 20, four miles west of Michigan City and fifty miles east of Chicago. Its postcard describes the cabins as steam-heated with innerspring mattresses, a restaurant and a filling station in connection. *Jane Simon Ammeson.*

"Where We Stop for Lunch and Rest, 22 Miles East of Broadway, Gary, 4 Miles West of Franklin St., Michigan City, on Dunes Highway, Route 12."

The Duck Inn was located just west of Michigan City, and like many roadside motels, it served food and had a gas station. *LaPorte Historical Society.*

BRYANT'S MOTEL ON HIGHWAY U.S. 12 — MICHIGAN CITY, IND. — PH. 2-4793

Bryant's Motel in Michigan City exemplifies the motel era that started in the 1920s. The era peaked in 1964, when there were sixty-one thousand throughout the country. That number then plummeted to around twelve thousand in 2009, and that number has only continued to dwindle. *LaPorte County Historical Society Museum.*

Water Sports, Shady Shores Resort, Dewey Lake, Dowagiac, Mich.   22

Shady Shores Resort was located on Dewey Lake, one of the popular Sister Lakes in Dowagiac, Michigan. *The Tichnor Brothers Collection, Boston Public Library.*

During the 1970s, Howard Johnson's had 929 restaurants and 526 motor lodges stretching across the United States. In the 1960s, the restaurants served more meals outside the home than any other company or organization, except for the U.S. Army.

There actually was a Howard Johnson (his middle name was Deering), and he was born in 1897. Although he liked to present himself, even at the height of his company's success, as a simple man, he married four times and owned a yacht, three houses and a substantial art collection. Oh, and the real Howard Johnson didn't really eat at Howard Johnson's much. Instead, he liked dining at high-end French restaurants, like Le Pavillon and the Stork Club, both fancy and ultra-expensive New York restaurants. And in an interesting twist, his former line cook, Jacques Pépin, went on to be the executive chef at Le Pavillon.

Barbecue was a frequent item on restaurant menus, as was fried chicken. These motor courts, unlike the Vista Grande in Stevensville, were typically cozy-looking places where the wife made meals while the husband oversaw other aspects of running the business. Sometimes, these small mom-and-pop places would advertise "no men in the kitchen" as a selling point.

Drive-ins started popping up as well. According to the University of Michigan, in 1921, two men, J.G. Kirby and Dr. Reuben W. Jackson, revolutionized the restaurant industry by introducing one of the first drive-

Terry's Drive-In in LaPorte County. *LaPorte County Historical Society*.

Bob's Barbeque was located in Rolling Prairie Indiana, 71 miles east of Chicago, 175 miles west of Toledo and 200 miles west of Detroit. *LaPorte County Historical Society*.

"As Indiana's finest modern equipped cabins and restaurants," Bob's Barbeque, at the junction of Routes 7 and 20, advertised twenty-four-hour service. *LaPorte County Historical Society.*

The ice cream shop at the House of David Park. *Benton Harbor Public Library.*

Left: The front of the menu of Bonnie Doon Drive-in. *The History Museum.*

Below: Bonnie Doon Drive-In's menu. *The History Museum.*

ICE CREAM

Ice Cream Flavors
Black Cherry, Blue Moon, Bubblegum, Chocolate, Chocolate Almond, Chocolate Chip, Crummy Cookie, Lemon Custard, Mint, Mint Chip, Orange Sherbet, Peanut Butter, Pecan Krunch, Strawberry, or Vanilla. *Seasonal Flavors, too!*

Le Doon Low-Fat Frozen Yogurt Flavors
Banana, Doonberry, Plain, Raspberry, Strawberry, or Vanilla. *Seasonal Flavors, too! (.25 Extra Per Scoop)*

Syrups
Chocolate, Strawberry, Vanilla, Cherry, Green River, Lemon, Pineapple, Root Beer

Toppings
Hot Fudge, Butterscotch, Marshmallow, Peach, Cherry, Pineapple, Strawberry

Ice Cream Sodas
Choose from any flavor & syrup or try our famous Choco-Mint Soda!   Reg. 1.80   Large 2.40

Ice Cream Sundaes
Create your own with any flavor and topping! You'll love our Hot Fudge Sundae!
Kiddie 1.50   Reg. 1.80   Large 2.65
Nut Topping .... .25 Extra *It's worth it!*
Tin Roof .... Reg. 1.95 Large 2.75
   Made with vanilla ice cream, chocolate syrup & Spanish peanuts.

Banana Boat
With 2-Dips of your favorite flavor 2.35
With 3-Dips 2.80

Cones & Dishes
Single .90   Double Dip 1.50   Sugar Cones .10 Extra

Floats
Try it with Root Beer!
Reg. 1.70   Large 2.30

Hand Dipped Malts & Shakes
Made the good old fashioned way .
MALTS
Small   Reg.   Large
1.90   2.50   2.95
SHAKES
1.70   2.30   2.75

Packaged Ice Cream
Pint 1.39
Quart-Party Slices   2.59
Quart 2.09
Quart-Frozen
   Yogurt 2.99
Half Gallon 3.19
Gallon Pail Vanilla   4.89
3 Gallons 12.99

★ *Pint of Bonnie Doon ice cream free with a RED STAR on your receipt!*

— *Senior Citizen discount available.* —

SANDWICHES, ETC.

	Sandwiches	Platters
Bonnie Burger	2.35	3.60
Hamburger	1.30	2.55
Cheeseburger	1.50	2.75
Bacon Cheeseburger	2.15	3.40
Bonnie Dog	1.25	2.50
Coney Dog	1.75	3.00
Fish Fillet	1.85	3.10
Chicken Fillet	1.75	3.00
Grilled Cheese	1.25	2.50
B.L.T.	1.70	2.95
Ham & Cheese	1.90	3.15
Chicken Salad	1.60	2.85
Tuna Salad	1.65	2.90
Pork Tenderloin	1.80	3.05
Grilled Chicken Breast	2.60	3.85

Salads
Tuna or Chicken Salad & Tomato Wedges on a bed of lettuce .. 2.00
Tossed Salad with Ham & Cheese.......... 2.00
Cottage Cheese with Tomato Wedges or Peach Slices...... 1.50

Platters served with your choice of any two of the following: French Fries, Applesauce, Cottage Cheese, Coleslaw or Peach Slices.

Soups & Sides
Chili............ Cup 1.10
                   Bowl 1.60
Soup .... Cup 1.00
                   Bowl 1.50
Fried Mushrooms .. 1.25
Onion Rings 1.25
French Fries 1.10
Applesauce......... .75
Peach Slices........ .75
Cottage Cheese ..... .75
Coleslaw .... .75

Beverages
Soft Drinks .80 1.00 1.25
Phosphates .80 1.00 1.25
   Try a Green River!
Coffee/Decaf......... .70
   Brewed
Ice Tea .80 1.00 1.25
Brewed Hot Tea ... .70

Milk.................. .70 .95
   White, Chocolate
Juice.................... 1.00
   Tomato, Orange
Hot Chocolate,
   in season .... .70
Lemonade,
   in season .80 1.00 1.25

in eateries in the country. Called the Texas Pig Stand, the barbecue-themed restaurant with curbside service was located off a busy highway in Dallas, Texas. Customers sat in their automobiles and, uniquely, instead of girls on roller skates, tray boys delivered barbecue pork and Coca-Colas. J.G. Kirby is quoted as saying, "People with cars are so lazy, they don't want to get out of them to eat."

Another early drive-in was A&W, which became the nation's first chain (way before McDonald's), and by the early 1930s, it had 171 restaurants throughout the country. Currently there are 492. California is the state with the most A&W restaurants. Michigan has 40, and Indiana has about 8.

4
HOUSE OF DAVID

The House of David story has fascinated the minds of millions for over a century," wrote Chris Siriano, the owner and curator of the House of David Museum in Saint Joseph, Michigan, about this religious organization founded and headquartered in Benton Harbor. "It was a place in Michigan that was surrounded by mystery, religion, romance, baseball, travel, sex (or lack thereof), scandal, and huge wealth. It was all based on an unusual religious colony that called themselves the House of David. Their leader and founder, Benjamin Purnell, preached that he was teaching the way to have eternal life of the body and the way to live forever on Earth."

Siriano continued:

> Converts traveled from afar to hear the message and many would join the colony, giving up worldly possessions in exchange for the promise of everlasting life. They came from all corners of the globe to see what they were being told was paradise on earth. Those that joined spoke of feeling like they were at the gates of heaven as they arrived to trumpets and bands playing, everyone extravagant. Retire, behold horse and carriages, and magnificent, magnificent, elaborate mansions to call home. They flocked in by the thousands and many would make their lives there forever.

King Benjamin (1861–1927), as he was known, was married to Mary Purnell (1862–1953), and they came to Benton Harbor in 1903 from Fostoria, Ohio. They had preached their religious philosophy in other towns,

The Golden Fountain is one of several healthy springs located on the properties of the House of David and, across the street, Mary's City of David just on Britain Avenue in Benton Harbor. The mineral springs fad took hold in Southwest Michigan and brought thousands seeking healthy waters. *Benton Harbor Public Library*.

but for some reason, it resonated here. Within four years, the House of David Colony (also known as the Israelite House of David) had several hundred members and had acquired about one thousand acres, many of which were used for growing fruits, vegetables and grains. It was a self-contained, self-sufficient religious group with its own bakery, cannery, carpenter shop, coach factory, steam laundry, tailor shop and print shop. The colony also owned and operated an electric plant. It also owned a five-thousand-acre island off the shores of northwest Michigan, where it grew crops as well.

But the leaders also understood the value of tourism, and they knew that to make money, they needed to offer fun. There was a train, a barnstorming baseball team that was very good, three brass bands, two orchestras, an ice cream parlor, zoological gardens, a dance hall, tiny cars for kids to ride and several mineral springs. Add to that live entertainment in the park, cottages, a hotel and even a Romanian rabbi to conduct services for Romanians from Chicago who summered at the cottages owned by the House of David.

The interior of the Park Restaurant on the grounds of the House of David. *Benton Harbor Public Library.*

Mary's Restaurant, a vegetarian restaurant in Benton Harbor. *Benton Harbor Public Library.*

A 1914 article in the *Chicago Tribune* lauded Purnell's genius at mass-mailing advertising, noting, "He mailed out thousands of books and pamphlets to prospective converts in all parts of the world." Many came.

Siriano, who has long had an avid interest in local history and who spent weekends at the park with his parents when he was young, also admires the business acumen of those who ran the park and how they created a major tourism draw. According to one newspaper account, by 1925, the baseball team was bringing in $125,000 a year.

The colony's commitment to vegetarianism came from the Gospels, as Taylor points out in his book by quoting biblical passages, including, "Meats of the belly and the belly for meats and both shall be destroyed," (1 Cor. 6:13).

Mary's City of David also attracted a large clientele of visitors who spent the summer in the numerous cottages on the property. "The cottages didn't have cooking facilities," said Taylor, "and so people ate at the restaurant."

The whole experience was unique. Farm-to-table cooking, sourcing locally and vegetarianism are all major food trends now, but one hundred years ago and more, abstaining from meat was very rare indeed.

But it worked. Eden Springs Park Restaurant (opened in 1908 and closed in 1932), Mary's Vegetarian Restaurant (opened in 1932 and closed thirty-four years later) and Mary's Café (in business from 1931 to 1975 in downtown Benton Harbor) were all very popular.

"GOOD MUSIC. GOOD BEER. GOOD FOOD."

An advertisement in the June 22, 1935 edition of the *Herald Palladium* touted Saturday night entertainment with Chic Bell and his Symphonic Dance Orchestra at 8:00 p.m., followed by dancing at the open-air beer garden. On Sunday afternoon, the Ladies' Band, under the direction of Krake, was performing.

The produce served in these establishments was grown and harvested by members on the farm.

Taylor credits the freshness of the ingredients with the longtime popularity of the restaurants. Taylor, who worked at Mary's Café for the last four years of its existence, has long been an archivist of the colony's history. Several years ago, he reprinted a limited edition of the 1912 cookbook titled *Vegetarian Cookbook*, which has recipes from the Eden Springs Restaurant. That was soon followed by another cookbook he edited, *Vegetarian Cook*

Mary's Restaurant advertised "meals at all hours." *Benton Harbor Public Library*.

Book, which includes not only the recipes from the 1934 cookbook but also photographs and historic anecdotes from the years when Mary's City of David had its own bakery, dairy, cannery, chickens (for eggs) and orchards. "We had a greenhouse for growing vegetables in the winter," said Taylor, an avid historian dedicated to preserving the unique history of the community.

A 1940 menu from the restaurant features such items as Belgian waffles for $0.50 and the Eden Springs Special (a tomato stuffed with egg salad and garnished with Queen green olives, accompanied by celery in a lettuce cup and mayonnaise). Luncheon (that's what they called it) offerings came with rolls, butter and a beverage and included such dishes as vegetable chop suey with noodles and hot mock hamburger with mashed potatoes and gravy, both of which cost $0.75. Baked macaroni was sold for $0.65. Sometime during that decade, the restaurant's prices went up—the price for mock hamburger rose to $1.25 but now included a salad as well as the rolls, butter and a beverage, and several items were added, including the mock club sandwich, made with mock meat, fried egg, sliced tomato, and lettuce on toast with chips and garnish for $1.35. There was no longer a Belgium waffle for $0.50; instead, a Belgium pancake with jelly cost $1.00.

The employees at Mary's Café in Benton Harbor, one of several vegetarian restaurants in the city. *Benton Harbor Public Library.*

A ticket for the train ride at the House of David Park. *Benton Harbor Public Library.*

Looking through the window at diners in Mary's Restaurant. *Benton Harbor Public Library.*

The prices were somewhat reduced at the House of David's Beer Garden when, according to a 1943 menu, mock steak was sold for twenty-five cents and a glass of Schlitz or Miller's High Life cost a quarter. For forty-five cents, you could get a quart of Schlitz. But for those who wanted to spend less, the obvious choice was Drewry's, which was on draught for ten cents. Wines by the glass, such as blackberry, Sauterne, Muscatel and Burgundy, would set you back twenty cents.

A 1947–48 menu from Mary's Restaurant shows shockingly cheap prices compared to restaurants today. A pimento cheese sandwich cost twenty cents, a slice of homemade pie or cake cost ten cents and spaghetti in tomato and cheese sauce would set a diner back thirty-five cents. For those who often splurge on lattes or cappuccinos, take note that a cup of coffee with extra cream cost fifteen cents, while something called Boston coffee was also sold for fifteen cents.

The same decade saw the publication of the *House of David Cookbook: Good Food Creates Health*, which features recipes for two different nut dishes—English walnut and nut roast, mock steak and soybean sausage. The mock steak was an interesting mixture of peanut butter, parsley, grated American cheese, brown beans, boiled carrots, fried onions, eggs, walnut and peanuts, breadcrumbs and assorted seasonings, all blended

Inside the House of David restaurant in the park. *Benton Harbor Public Library.*

together and then molded into steaks. That recipe produced eighty-five steaks, which seems like a lot.

The year 1951 saw the release of *The House of David Vegetarian Recipes*, published by the House of David, which also emphasized the need for people to make sure they had enough vitamins and minerals in their diets. The cookbook also has a plethora of easy-to-make—if somewhat uncommon—recipes, like carrot nut loaf, chestnut rolls, welsh rarebit, rinktum ditty (a mixture of sautéed onions, tomatoes, cheese and eggs served on toast points) and nut brown vegetable pie.

"This is a book of recipes," wrote Taylor, who joined the organization in 1977. "It continues authentic and unique tastes of a history from a community of that generation. It was designed to serve a healthy and nutritious meal for the working class. Convenience to a fresh market of local produce precluded the use of exotic ingredients and thus retained the colony's desire to make an affordable and family friendly menu. It remains a book of ingredients that saw its popularity within the era of one of America's greatest generations."

But there was trouble in paradise. The House of David, it was alleged, had a sinister side. King Ben and some of the other male leaders were accused of subjecting young girls to "marriages." A series of court cases and a state investigation into these alleged "immoralities" were covered extensively in not only local newspapers but the national press as well. King Ben died before judgement was passed. Queen Mary, obviously not pleased, created Mary's City of David and moved across the street. It, too, believed in self-sufficiency.

As for King Ben, his body is said to remain in a glass coffin. I have talked to two people who have seen it, but it's not on any tour.

Before the split, the House of David had about six hundred members, all of whom believed King Ben's prophecy that the world was soon coming to an end and thus the pleasures of the flesh should be denied here to gain salvation. Because sex was prohibited, if husbands and wives joined, they couldn't live together and instead became "brothers" and "sisters."

"What did it matter to them, since the end date was coming soon?" said Siriano when explaining why people would abstain from not only romantic relationships but also tobacco and alcohol. Nor did they cut their hair. This was done because, as the *Chicago Tribune* reported one member saying, the hair helped channel electricity from the air. But this really doesn't explain why they needed an electrical plant.

The outdoor theater at the House of David Park. *St. Joseph Public Library*.

Unfortunately, the end date, continued Siriano, kept getting pushed forward, and even though there was continuing threat that the world would soon end, Mary's City of David acquired the unfinished hotel in downtown Benton Harbor in the division of colony assets, and her members finished it. It was remarkably modern for its day; two-thirds of the guest rooms featured private baths instead of having a shared bath down the hall. Despite opening in the depths of the Great Depression, the hotel and Mary's City of David Vegetarian Café, located on the first floor, enjoyed immediate success. As an interesting aside, according to historian Bob Myers, the hotel gained fame for its glittering exterior, which was made with the Israelites' own patented sparkling concrete. The restaurant was open until 1975, but by then, the communes were running out of members.

VISTA GRANDE

This swank and elaborate resort with a Southwestern vibe similar to the missions found in California, New Mexico and Arizona opened in 1935 in Stevensville, south of Saint Joseph. It was another winning business fostered by the commune.

Large enough to accommodate 150 overnight guests, Vista Grande was the ultimate in motor courts, with forty apartments, each with a private garage. Splashing water erupted from the center fountain, and rocks and minerals, like sparkling quartz, along with relics from New Mexico, added to the ambience of being in America's southwest.

The two-story lounge, with its painted ceilings and an Art Moderne–style bar with bartenders in white tuxedos, a dance floor and cigarette girls in gold lame, was unlike any other motor court in Michiana. There was also a gas station with uniformed attendants and an auto garage with a Streamline Moderne flair.

It was such a hit that within two years, a quarter of a million people had spent at least one night at the resort, and thousands more had dined there or danced to the live band in the nightclub. An addition was built to double its size. It was, according to an article in the *Herald Press*, one of the largest and finest tourist courts in the United States.

In the beginning the restaurant just served vegetarian fare, that changed in 1939, when the restaurant and its gardens were leased to H. Edgar Gregory of Chicago, who added meat dishes. Popular with both locals and visitors from Chicago and South Bend, it was probably the fanciest nightclub

The Vista Grande in Stevensville was so successful that within two years, the owners had doubled the number of rooms. *Benton Harbor Public Library*.

Vista Grande was considered one of the largest and most luxurious motor courts in the United States. *Benton Harbor Public Library*.

Touted as the most luxurious motor court in the country, the Vista Grande even had cigarette girls (as they were called back then) in its swank restaurant. It advertised steak, chicken and fish dinners, along with dancing, in 1940. C.H. Lyon was the proprietor. *Benton Harbor Public Library*.

Even the filling station at the Vista Grande in Stevensville looked stylish and glamorous. It advertised accommodations for auto parties, a garage for autos, gasoline and oil and said, "Chicago Dinners Our Specialty." *Benton Harbor Public Library.*

Bartenders in white tuxedos were not the standard in tiny Stevensville, south of St. Joseph, but they were at the Vista Grande, which was advertised as a "Beautiful Shady Place Near Lake and River," where "Special Attention [was] Given to Tourists." *Benton Harbor Public Library.*

around. Business was good for decades, but time always takes its toll, and all traces of Vista Grande are now gone.

Siriano, who, for years, gave tours of the grounds, including the opulent Shiloh and Diamond House, talks about what remains. The thirty-two-thousand-square-foot Shiloh House has 102 rooms, and the nine-thousand-square-foot Diamond House is super ornate. "There are rooms with rooms, hidden passageways, and moving walls," said Siriano, who helped lead a multimillion dollar restoration project.

Now known as Eden Springs Park, the grounds of the House of David are open for tours, and the train runs on a schedule, even at Christmastime.

5
AL CAPONE IN MICHIANA

On Saturday, December 14, 1929, Saint Joseph city police officer Charles Skelly jumped on the running board of a Hudson coupe, which had been involved in a minor accident, directing the driver to the police station. But Fred Dane had a different agenda. Just as the stoplight turned green, he pulled out a Colt .45 and shot Skelly. Then he roared away.

It was a mortal shot, and though two firemen donated blood to Skelly as he lay dying at the Saint Joseph Sanitarium, all efforts were futile. His last words to his fellow officers before he died were: "Get that guy."

That guy's real name was Fred "Killer" Burke. While searching his home in Stevensville, police discovered $300,000 in cash (about $5,260,500 in 2023) and a machine gun that was used in the infamous Saint Valentine's Day Massacre.

"Nobody kills like that but Capone," a rival gangster was quoted as saying about the Valentine's Day slaying of six members of the Bugs Moran Gang and a luckless bystander. Moran had unwisely hijacked some of Capone's booze. Obviously, that couldn't be allowed to go unpunished. Known to meet up at the S-M-C Cartage Co. garage north of downtown Chicago every morning, Capone sent four of his henchmen, including two dressed as policemen, to take out his rival. Luckily for Moran, he hadn't made it to the garage yet, but seven of his men who were there were out of luck. Thinking it was a police raid, they lined up against the wall as ordered. But there was no arrest. Machine guns were pulled, lots of bullets flew and all seven died.

In 1929, Vincent Bendix, the founder of the Bendix Aviation Corporation, purchased 610 acres northwest of South Bend. Called the Bendix Municipal Airport, it eventually became today's South Bend International Airport. Amelia Earhart landed her Lockheed Electra aircraft at Bendix Field in 1936. *The Tichnor Brothers Collection, Boston Public Library.*

Burke managed to escape the search, but he would ultimately be captured, returned to Michigan and sentenced to life in prison in 1931. He would die of a heart attack nine years later in the Michigan State Prison, the only mobster who served time for the massacre. But the big question is: Why was a Chicago thug hanging out in bucolic Michiana?

Well, according to historian and author Robert Myers, who speaks on the subject, even gangsters liked to get away from it all. Several Capone henchmen owned property locally. Besides Burke, Capone advisor Phil D'Andrea had a grand home (both homes remain but are now private residences) in Saint Joseph. That house came with a unique amenity—a tunnel that led out into the Saint Joseph River. Maybe it was used for alcohol deliveries? After all, Canada isn't that far away, and alcohol was legal there. Or maybe it was used for a quick escape. Probably both.

When they were here, the mobsters, including Capone and his gang, enjoyed the leisure activities typical of any tourist. They played golf, dined out, went to the House of David Amusement Park and enjoyed taking mineral baths at places like the Dwan and the Whitcomb Hotels. The Whitcomb has special structural glass that did not discolor from the sulfa and sulfur of their mineral waters. The glass also absorbed and retained heat, which meant warm floors and dressing rooms at all times.

Some who claim to know say that Capone convinced a fellow gang member to raise money for the construction of the Hotel Vincent, a luxurious, eight-story hotel in downtown Benton Harbor—and we're pretty sure that when mobsters go asking for donations, it's hard to say no. The 151-room Vincent, which is still standing, was quite the place— starting with the bowling alley in the basement. There were main and private dining rooms, two elevators, a ballroom with maple flooring, lots and lots of marble, thick carpeting and gleaming wood. For the Vincent's grand opening, chef Stephen Loth spent twenty hours crafting a four-foot-tall model of the hotel out of sugar blocks held together with sugar mortar.

Whether Capone bankrolled the building of the Vincent or not, the *Herald Palladium* mentioned he frequented the place. They liked him there. He was polite and tipped everyone generously—the barbers, the elevator operators, clerks and bussers, as well as the servers at the Hotel Vincent Café. "When Capone comes here, he's just a guest and nothing more," said

The Hotel Vincent, located on Main Street in downtown Benton Harbor on the side of the Princess Theatre, was one of the places said to be frequented by Al Capone and his gang. *Benton Harbor Public Library.*

Premier Mineral Baths in Benton Harbor announced that starting in November 1928, it would be keeping its men's mineral bath and massage departments open every evening until midnight from then on. Business was so good that the Premier built an addition in the 1920s. *Benton Harbor Public Library.*

Though it's no longer a hotel, this building and others are still standing in Higman Park in Benton Harbor. *The Tichnor Brothers Collection, Boston Public Library.*

Dan O'Connor, the hotel's manager. He went on to add that he'd never had any complaints about the legendary gangster or his friends.

According to David Critchley, the author of *Gangsters in Southwest Michigan*, the *News-Palladium* complained, "Capone's presence has become so matter-of-fact here that the local citizenry, refusing to get excited about the proximity of one more headliner, has ceased to pay much attention to the comings and goings of Capone's fleet of 16-cylinder sedans."

It also helped that Prohibition was very unpopular, and people like Capone made sure that speakeasies and "soda" shops in the region didn't run dry.

Capone and his men were also on their best behavior at the Greenland Inn, an Italian restaurant on Paw Paw Avenue and Riverside Road. "They tipped big, very big," said Siriano, whose grandparents Sam and Jennie Siriano opened the inn in 1928. The restaurant would remain in the family until the early 1960s, and then it was sold, becoming the Joker's Club. "But they didn't want anyone sitting near them; they didn't want anything they said to be overheard," he continued. Siriano, a realtor who also owns and operates the House of David Museum in Saint Joseph, said, "They enjoyed themselves and my grandparents never had any problems with them."

At the time, Benton Harbor had a large Italian population, with a neighborhood where many lived called Brooklyn. Sam Siriano was the president of the Italian American Club. Jennie Siriano cooked Italian dishes such as spaghetti, ravioli, Italian steaks and Italian baked chicken for patrons of her restaurant.

According to Siriano, Capone struck up a deal with the leaders of the House of David to help them obtain a liquor license once Prohibition ended in 1933. Even though members of the House of David were forbidden from drinking (sex was taboo as well, which is probably a major factor in why the membership is now almost zero), but they weren't adverse to serving alcohol. "The House of David received the first liquor license in Michigan after Prohibition ended," said Siriano. "They were very astute businesspeople." And people were very thirsty.

REMEMBER COLD DUCK? TURNS out the biggest producer of Cold Duck was Bronte Winery in Hartford, Michigan. The winery opened in 1933, shortly before the repeal of Prohibition. At one point, it was the most productive winery in the state, turning out eight hundred thousand gallons per year.

But there's a Capone component here as well. According to the FotoGuy49057, who posted on Flickr:

Cypress wine storage tanks from Al Capone's Kankakee, Illinois, brewery were situated in the main cellar of the winery. A total of 44 cypress and oak aging tanks held 15,000 gallons of wine each and seven glass-lined tanks held 20,000 gallons each. [An] Italian winemaker, who is legendary, planted Baco Noir, a French-American hybrid grape, and produced the state's first commercial wine from a French-American hybrid in 1954. In all, Bronte had more than 70,000 vines. Bronte is now closed.

Capone and other gangsters stayed at Pleasant Grove (now the Lakeside Inn) in Lakeside, Michigan. It was probably both business and pleasure at this attractive inn that is still in business. According to Dianna Stampfler, a historian, travel expert and author, bootleggers were said to dock their boats in front of the inn, where guests would help unload the cases of booze that were served inside or taken to sell at other locations.

Though many of the big distilleries had to close their doors with the advent of Prohibition, putting tens of thousands of people out of work, what liquor couldn't be imported from Canada, where it was still legal, was

A St. Julian Winery delivery truck. St. Julian Winery was founded before Prohibition and is still in business today, located in Paw Paw, Michigan. *St. Julian Winery.*

made in the United States. And Southwest Michigan, with its abundance of grains (wheat, corn and rye), ripe fruit for wines and brandy and isolated small farms tucked on unpaved rural roads, was the perfect location for bootleggers. But a single still wasn't going to keep up with demand. So, bootleggers set up small distilleries to increase the flow of production.

Profits were great but so were the risks for both restaurant and hotel owners who sold alcohol during Prohibition and those who manufactured it.

B.A. Boswell, the proprietor of the European and Gem Hotels in Benton Harbor, was convicted of bootlegging in September 1926, after a witness testified that he purchased peach brandy at the Gem Hotel. "I had to do it," Boswell told the court when explaining why he sold liquor even though it was illegal. "Every other hotel is, and I couldn't keep the trade if I didn't."

Boswell was probably fined. For those who made hooch, the stakes were much higher.

On Friday, April 27, 1927, the *Herald Palladium* reported two major hauls of illegal liquor. Sheriff Fred G. Bryant and his deputies raided the farm on Riverside Road, owned by Tony and Mary Domingo, confiscating 118 gallons of sugar moonshine, around 13,000 gallons of mash, eleven 1,000 gallon vats, a number of barrels used for storing mash and both a huge upright boiler and stove and other distillery equipment.

A postcard of the Vista Grande. *Benton Harbor Public Library.*

Around the same time, more sheriff's deputies conducted a raid on Hilltop Farm, located a mile and a half northeast of Twelve Corners. Here, deputies discovered three 10-gallon stills that were hooked up to a huge upright boiler and eleven 1,000-gallon vats filled with mash. In all, the distillery was capable of producing 240 gallons of liquor daily, making it the largest ever seized in Berrien County and one of the largest in the state. Domingo was arrested, but Leo Ciaravino, the owner of Hilltop Farm, was nowhere to be found. He had most likely gotten a phone call that told him the deputies were on their way.

Ominously, while the deputies were at work dismantling Ciaravino's contraptions, a line of large black cars appeared on the perimeter, circling the farm over and over. Fearful of an attack and knowing they were outnumbered, the deputies called the sheriff, who was at the Domingo distillery. Bryant grabbed some shotguns, picked up several police officers and a railroad detective and sped to the scene with reinforcements. If the mobsters had planned an attack, this was enough to deter them, and the distillery and its equipment were taken to the county jail and the mash was destroyed.

Things were going to get a lot worse for Tony.

"Bootleg Feud Bomb Kills Italian Woman: Rival Faction Bombs Car; Husband Starts Gun War," read the headline of the October 22, 1927 edition of the *Saint Joseph Herald-Press*. Two months after the raid, a bomb under the hood of the car Mary Domingo was driving detonated, destroying the vehicle. Her mutilated body was found fifteen feet away.

Upon being told that Louie Veregilo was responsible for the murder, Tony and his brother Sebastiano grabbed their shotguns and headed to the Fourth Ward Italian Political Club in Benton Harbor, where the killer was said to be. Veregilo managed to escape the gunfire, and the brothers were arrested.

The Ciaravinos and the Domingos were related through marriage and careers. Many of them met similar ends.

Tony sold the farm and moved back to Chicago. Violence followed him, and he was shot nine times while eating dinner at a restaurant owned by Pasquale Spilotro. Tony's brother Sebastiano was murdered in 1933 while playing cards at the Castle Café at 72 East First Street in New York City. One other man died in the barrage, and four were injured. According to author David Critchley, the shooters shouted, "You dirty bunch of rats!"

Spilotro's son Tony "The Ant" Spilotro, who was played by Joe Pesci in the movie *Casino*, also met an untimely end. He and his brother, Michael, were found buried, wearing only their shorts, in a cornfield in Northwest Indiana. They'd been beaten to death.

But Southwest Michigan wasn't the only area in Michiana where Capone spent time. He sometimes had business in Mishawaka, and while he was there, he would stop in at the Midway Tavern—only it wasn't called that during Prohibition. In order to stay in business, the owners substituted Lunch for Tavern. But they kept serving booze. Once Prohibition was over, the name changed again.

The joint, still in business, was owned by Cyril and Martha Anthenius, who bought the place in 1924, when it still had dirt floors and a pot-bellied stove. One of their customers, Martha, who had immigrated from Holland, didn't know who Capone was, but he would bring her a dozen roses every time he stopped by. She thought he was good-looking and nice. Little did she know he was a notorious gangster.

Martha made hooch and also bought some from a nearby farm. When a customer wanted booze, which was kept in the garage out back, she'd put the glass in her apron pocket and go get some. Customers could also drink near beer (legal) for five cents, eat a pork sandwich for ten cents or go all out and order the chicken for twenty-five cents. Busted in 1930, the place was padlocked by the police. The family moved to Holland for nine months, returned and reopened. After Prohibition finally ended in 1933, the

The Swedish Coffee Pot advertised "Swedish food the way it should taste" and was located in Harbert, Michigan, which had a large Swedish population. *Jane Simon Ammeson.*

owners added air conditioning, a floor, booths and a stage. Other than that, not much has changed. It has good jazz and good food and is now called Martha's Midway Tavern. Martha worked there for sixty-six years. She lived to the age of ninety-one and was featured on CNN and in *People* magazine. She was also inducted into the Bartender's Hall of Fame. I mean, how could you not visit this place?

6
CHOP SUEY, SWEDISH PANCAKES, SAUERBRATEN AND PIEROGI

From the Swedes, Lithuanians and Bohemians who settled in the southwest corner of Berrien County in Michigan to the Germans and Italians farther north in Michiana and the large Polish population in South Bend. Indeed, South Bend residents still celebrate Dyngus Days and local bakeries turn out thousands of paczkis on Fat Tuesday. That's the day when all the items not allowed during Lent are consumed before Ash Wednesday.

Chop suey restaurants—or "joints," as they were often called—proliferated in the United States in the early 1900s. They were popularized by the many Chinese who came to America in the 1800s to work on such big projects as the construction of the railroads and working in mining camps. They also ran businesses that catered to the workers, such as restaurants and trading posts.

In 1905, C.H. Chan of Chicago opened an American and Chinese restaurant at the corner of Ship and State Streets in St. Joseph. Short orders comprised both American and Chinese dishes, and Chan assured readers of the *Saint Joseph Daily Press* that "Everything [was] first class and up-to-date Chicago style."

Chop suey restaurants—and, around the turn of the last century, they mostly were chop suey joints, not Asian restaurants—offered cheap food and were typically open until late at night. Such was the Chop Suey and Chinese Café (open from 2:00 p.m. until 2:00 a.m.), which advertised it was for both ladies and gentlemen at the Standard Hotel in the *Elkhart Weekly-Truth* on February 28, 1907.

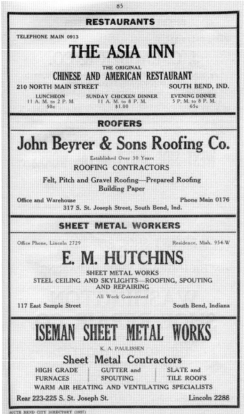

Above: Note the sign painted on the building advertising Chop Suey on the left-hand side of this photograph of downtown Benton Harbor. *St. Joseph Public Library*.

Left: An advertisement in the *South Bend City Directory* for the Asia Inn on North Main Street in South Bend. *The History Museum*.

"To Serve Chop Suey" was the lead for a small news article in the April 19, 1907 *Goshen Weekly News Times*. The headline was followed by the information that Ralph Miller, the proprietor of the Jefferson Café, would begin, on Saturday night, serving chop suey every night. "Mr. Miller spent three months in a Chinese restaurant in New York City. He will serve three kinds, the American, Chinese, and chicken."

"Chop Suey! Chop Suey!" was the headline for an advertisement in the *Goshen Democrat* on December 18, 1908, announcing that, starting Saturday, the Interurban Lunchroom, so-called because it was located beneath the interurban station, would be serving not only lunch and short orders, but it would also add chop suey for twenty cents, twenty-five cents and fifty cents.

In 1908, the Chinese Chop Suey Restaurant at Silver Beach advertised first-class Chinese and Japanese dishes, as well as good tea.

Kan Ying Lo's Chinese Chop Suey Restaurant was located on the second floor at the corner of Ship and State Streets in 1909.

"When you Go to Elkhart, be sure and visit the Republic Chop Suey Restaurant and get some of those delicious Chinese dishes that you hear your neighbors talking about. And take some home to your family. 526½ S. Main St., (upstairs) Elkhart. Phone 1216. Just across the street from the Electric Hardware," read an advertisement.

In 1917, W.H. Thomas and M.V. Fetters were the proprietors of a chop suey café at 134½ Main Street in Goshen.

"When you get tired of home cooking and want something different or when unexpected company drops in for supper, just come or send to Elkhart and get some Real Chinese Chop Suey and please the whole family at the Republic Restaurant, 526½ S. Main Street, just a little south of Hotel Elkhart."

The Golden Eagle Inn at 208–10 South Michigan Street in South Bend, Indiana, was a chop suey restaurant. It had a special Saturday dinner: half of a spring chicken for seventy-five cents, served from 5:00 p.m. to 9:00 p.m. Every evening, it had a five-piece orchestra. There were many American menus that cost seventy-five cents per plate. They often featured soup chicken á la Reine, a choice of half of a spring chicken fried with green peas, beach beef tenderloin broiled á la Stanly, jumbo fried eggs fried in a supreme sauce, veal cutlets with fresh mushrooms and pork chops broiled with candied sweet potatoes. These dinners were accompanied by cauliflower and cream. Mashed potatoes, a combination salad with French dressing and tea, coffee or milk was also served. And for dessert,

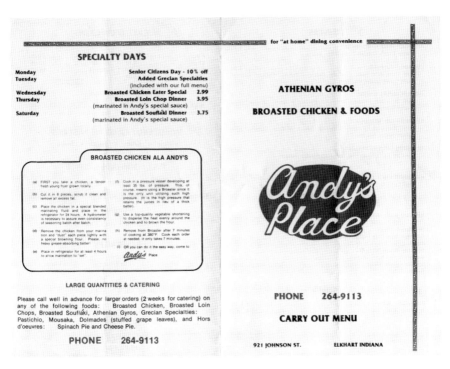

for "at home" dining convenience

SPECIALTY DAYS

Monday	Senior Citizens Day - 10% off	
Tuesday	Added Grecian Specialties	
	(included with our full menu)	
Wednesday	Broasted Chicken Eater Special	2.99
Thursday	Broasted Loin Chop Dinner	3.95
	(marinated in Andy's special sauce)	
Saturday	Broasted Souflaki Dinner	3.75
	(marinated in Andy's special sauce)	

BROASTED CHICKEN ALA ANDY'S

(a) FIRST you take a chicken, a tender fresh young fryer grown locally.

(b) Cut it in 8 pieces, scrub it clean and remove all excess fat.

(c) Place the chicken in a special blended marinating fluid and place in the refrigerator for 24 hours. A hydrometer is necessary to assure even consistancy of seasoning batch after batch.

(d) Remove the chicken from your marination and "dust" each piece lightly with a special browning flour. Please: no heavy grease-absorbing batter!

(e) Place in refrigerator for at least 4 hours to allow marination to "set".

(f) Cook in a pressure vessel developing at least 35 lbs. of pressure. This, of course, means using a Broaster since it is the only unit utilizing such high pressure. (It is the high pressure that retains the juices in lieu of a thick batter).

(g) Use a top-quality vegetable shortening to disperse the heat evenly around the chicken and to brown the flour.

(h) Remove from Broaster after 7 minutes of cooking at 380°F. Cook each order at needed, it only takes 7 minutes.

(i) OR you can do it the easy way, come to Andy's Place.

LARGE QUANTITIES & CATERING

Please call well in advance for larger orders (2 weeks for catering) on any of the following foods: Broasted Chicken, Broasted Loin Chops, Broasted Souflaki, Athenian Gyros, Grecian Specialties: Pastichio, Mousaka, Dolmades (stuffed grape leaves), and Hors d'oeuvres: Spinach Pie and Cheese Pie.

PHONE 264-9113

ATHENIAN GYROS

BROASTED CHICKEN & FOODS

Andy's Place

PHONE 264-9113

CARRY OUT MENU

921 JOHNSON ST. ELKHART INDIANA

Above: Andy's in Elkhart was a Greek diner. *The History Museum.*

Left: H.I.'s Old Towne Saloon was located in Niles, Michigan. There was also a H.I.'s on State Street in St. Joseph. Both were popular eating establishments in the 1970s and 1980s. *The History Museum.*

there was a homemade apple pie or ice cream. The restaurant's Chinese menu, which cost seventy-five cents per plate, featured chicken noodle soup, bean sprouts, egg foo young and fresh mushroom chop suey. This was accompanied by a bowl of rice, a pot of wo hop tea and Chinese almond cake. At the bottom of the advertisement, it read, "We also serve businessmen's lunch. From 11:00 to 2:00 PM. $0.50 per plate."

In 1923, the Hung Fong Restaurant in Benton Harbor opened, run by Chinese immigrants Joe Jue and George Jean and located across the street from the Liberty Theater. Arkie Chin, who immigrated from Hong Kong in 1938 and worked as a cook at the restaurant, purchased the business in 1958 from Jue and Jean. At one time, Chin recalled, the restaurant was so popular they had six waitresses and four cooks. Jin closed the restaurant in 1973.

South Bend News Times, Tuesday, March 10, 1914

"Open For Business"

Song Huey Low's Chinese restaurant served patrons both chop suey and American-style dishes at its new location over 110 South Michigan Street, four doors south of its former location. It was pleased to have its friends call in to see its new quarters. "Convince Yourself! We make good all our claims of having the complete up-to-date American and Chinese restaurant [at the Oriental Inn in South Bend]," read a 1916 advertisement.

The "Oriental" lunch comprised chop suey and cost thirty-five cents in 1916, and there was music in the evening at the newly remodeled Oriental Inn Café at 117 North Main Street, three doors north of the Oliver Hotel in South Bend.

In 1922, lunch at the South Bend Inn at 132 North Main Street cost forty-five cents, while dinner cost sixty-five cents. All diners received a free Chinese fan.

But running a chop suey place, with its cheap food and late hours, often attracted trouble.

ELKHART DAILY REVIEW, OCTOBER 2, 1908

"Caught in Chop Suey House: Elkhart Woman Fires Pistol Shot at Her Husband; Bartender Jealous of Her, Followed, When She Went With Sister 'to Call on a Friend.'"

When Mrs. Terey Hammer, the wife of the bartender at the Forrest Saloon in Elkhart, told her husband of about a year that she was going with her sister from Toledo to visit a friend, Hammer didn't buy it and tracked her down to a "chop suey" joint. After the couple returned home, they fought, and Mrs. Hammer (women didn't have first names back then as far as newspapers were concerned—and she's only referred to as Mrs. Terey Hammer or Mrs. Hammer) says he pushed her against the wall and choked her until she fell to the floor. Spying a gun on a dresser, she grabbed it and fired into the air to scare him.

The next morning, she charged him with assault and battery but later dismissed the proceeding. Hammer ordered her to leave, so she did, heading to her mother's in Indianapolis, along with the household effects and fifteen dollars in cash.

GOSHEN DAILY-DEMOCRAT, DECEMBER 9, 1916

"Fined $5 and Costs"

Henry R. Hatfield of Niles, Michigan, was fined five dollars and costs for raising a disturbance in a South Bend chop suey restaurant. He committed assault and battery on Miss Mamie Bankhead, a waitress.

SOUTH BEND-NEWS TIMES, MONDAY JUNE 18, 1917

"Melee in Chop Suey House Costs $6.25"

King Fong Lo, the proprietor of a chop suey restaurant at 128 South Michigan Street, testified that Frank Hilderbrand and Frank Kruger, both of Niles, started breaking dishes, chairs and chinaware in his restaurant, driving out his patrons, who fled without paying their bills. Though the men were found not guilty by the court, they were ordered to pay $6.25 to King Fong Lo, who had sought $10.00 in damages.

"The Chop Suey Mystery"

Frank Smigielski and Frank Boeye discovered a box of chop suey belonging to the Oriental Inn. The identity of the thieves was unknown.

SOUTH BEND NEWS-TIMES, FRIDAY, JUNE 11, 1920

"Someone Heaved a Rock Through the Chop Suey Window"

It seems that "certain dwellers in the Colfax Hotel" heaved a stone through the window and smashed the sign over the door of the South Bend Inn on North Main in South Bend.

WRITING IN *EDIBLE MICHIANA* magazine, Terry Mark remembered the Asian restaurant, Mark's Café in Elkhart, which his parents owned from the 1950s to the late '70s. "Back in the day, every Michiana family who had a Chinese restaurant knew one another," he recalled. "We kids? We called each other 'cousin,' even if we weren't actually related because, if nothing else, we shared a bond over busing tables, taking carryout orders over the phone and prepping vegetables."

He continued, "For the kids of my generation, the family business was a means to an end—a good education and stability—as we established ourselves. None of us work in food service today. Maybe our parents would have been proud if we had carried on the family business, but I have a feeling they would have been disappointed."

Mark's cousin Annie Mark spent hours in the kitchen at Happy House Restaurant, though she never got to cook the restaurant menu. "That was a job for her dad and uncle," he wrote. "But she remembers getting a kick out of her dad reading an order ticket and exclaiming, 'Oh, so-and-so is here tonight!'"

As for their own Thanksgiving dinners, which they invited regulars to join in on, there was turkey and dressing, roast duck, roast chicken, steamed white rice, shrimp chips ("Don't knock

A menu cover from the Oliver. *The History Museum.*

'em till you've tried 'em," Mark says), a spiced ham salad cheese ball and fried wontons. The latter, he says, he would have eaten by the ton, except there were adults watching.

In 1875, THE LOUIS Nickel Grocery at 228 West Washington Street had a German restaurant in the back.

An advertisement read, "Meals served at all hours at Oliver Café and gentleman's German room café."

In 1936, Krall's restaurant in South Bend was looking to hire a German or Hungarian cook.

On December 28, 1934, those looking for entertainment in Saint Joseph County, Indiana, could choose, for $2.50 a person, to enjoy a five-act floor show, an eight-course dinner and special dance music at the Palace Café at Michigan and Colfax Streets.

Otto's at 224 East Lasalle Avenue in South Bend featured good music, a stein of beer for five cents and a choice of two fried perch or sauerbraten with mashed potatoes. Either meal would set you back fifteen cents.

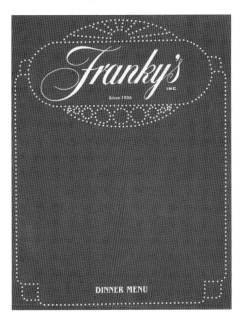

Left: Franky's, established in 1929, was a longtime favorite in Niles. *The History Museum*.

Right: Founded in 1908 by Frank Lenick, a butter maker by trade who expanded into distributing milk and soon had a popular ice cream shop as well. *LaPorte County Historical Society*.

Andy Kaufman's in South Bend was serving pork roast and sauerkraut on Friday December 17, 1888, but why anyone would want to eat at 9:30 when it was being served is beyond me.

Budapest Nights on Prairie Avenue was known for its wonderful Hungarian food.

On Saturday nights in 1911, Gus. H. Ebeling served sauerbraten at his restaurant on the corner of Colfax and Main Streets.

In 1936, Andy Riedel and his orchestra performed at the Hudson Lake Casino. General admission charges cost ladies twenty-five cents and gentlemen thirty-five cents. Fritz Drechsel was the manager, which might explain why you could get all the sauerbraten and potato pancakes you wanted for seventy-five cents (though all-you-could-eat spaghetti with meat or tomato sauce cost twenty-five cents). The restaurant also offered fish, steak and chicken dinners.

ELLINEE SOCIAL CENTER - PAW PAW LAKE, COLOMA, MICHIGAN   87756

Starting off as a peanut stand owned by Ernest H. Erickson, the Ellinee grew into a mega tourism complex with an art school, a one-hundred-foot-long pier into the lake, a three-lane bowling alley, a soda fountain, billiard tables and a dance floor with an electric player piano. The bill of fare at the Ellinee Village Inn in 1932 featured chicken, steak or fish dinners for one dollar. Frog legs would cost you an extra twenty-five cents. Dinner consisted of shrimp cocktail, a fruit bowl, a salad, a consommé and a choice of vegetables and French fries; dessert; and either beer or coffee. *St. Joseph Public Library.*

Pierogi were on the menu at Shire's Tavern (618 South Pulaski Street) in 1946 and 1947. The demand for what the advertisement described as "cheese turnovers" was so high that there was a note in the latter advertisement stating, "we appreciate your unusually heavy demand for pierogi the last two Fridays."

When Little Bohemia in New Buffalo was sold, the new owners changed the name of the restaurant to Hannah's, but they kept many of the original recipes, including former owner Elsie Kadlec's duck, slow cooked pot roast and dumplings, on the menu. The cuisine reflected the large Bohemia population in the area. But it's sadly out of business now. But Redamak's in New Buffalo is still open.

The Hans Haus, a German restaurant at 2803 South Michigan Street in South Bend, seated four hundred and served Bavarian-style food.

The Tuesday night specials at the Ranch House Cafeteria in Benton Harbor included stuffed cabbage, bratwurst, knockwurst (or Polish sausage), wiener schnitzel, liver dumplings with fried onions or fried chicken for $1.04 in 1968. Children's portions cost $0.60.

Frank Frucci Jr., a Pearl Harbor survivor who fought eighty-two missions as a gunner in a B-17 bomber in the battles of Midway and Guadalcanal and received numerous medals, including the Silver Star and the Air Medal with four oak leaf clusters, expanded the family-owned grocery store into Franky's Restaurant in Niles. *The History Museum.*

Every Thursday night, Horvath's El Tropico at 1528 Western Street served chicken parikas (we think that was a misspelling and it should be "paprika" or "paprikash") dinners with homemade noodles, rice and chicken giblets, along with its famous salad, coffee and dessert. Other menu items included steaks and seafood. Carl Horvath provided music nightly, playing the organ, piano and accordion.

In 1943, the Royal Café featured frog legs daily, had a fish fry on Friday nights and served Italian spaghetti with royal sauce on Wednesdays.

The Italian Village (2102 South Lafayette Street in South Bend), in 1949, advertised fish fries on Fridays. Other menu items included spaghetti, steak and chops. Pat Giantomaso and Bill De Luca were the proprietors.

For the Swedes who settled in Southwest Michigan, there was the Swedish Coffee Pot. They could get Swedish pancakes at Hyerdahl's in Bridgman and could feast on them at Andy Anderson's, 325 West Main Street in Benton Harbor, starting at 6:00 a.m. Other menu items included golden fried chicken, golden fried shrimp, Italian spaghetti, steaks cut to order and brook trout. "We bake our own pies and rolls," read the restaurant's advertisement in 1951.

Though it's not a restaurant, the Swedish Bakery in Harbert has been open for over seventy years, and Falatic's Meat Market in Sawyer, which has been around for decades, sells potato sausage and other Swedish items, particularly around Christmas time.

7
TIMES PAST

Food, Fun and Drink

If early pioneers and settlers were feasting on rabbit and squirrel, by the end of the nineteenth century, the fare being served in many restaurants was much more sophisticated—even more so than what we dine on today at some places.

An 1899 menu from the Elkerton in Dowagiac featured calves' sweetbreads, mushroom sauce and green peas, braised quail on toast with watercress, green turtle soup, filet of beef, sauce bordelaise and mashed potatoes, lobster salad and, for dessert, pistachio mottled cream, Roquefort cheese and assorted cake.

Hotel Dwan had both mineral baths and a coffee shop. In 1926, around the time of their peak popularity, the Premier, Saltzman and Dwan Hotel served twenty-five thousand guests and provided eighty-five thousand mineral baths. The Saltman Hotel originated as the Allmendinger Hotel and was built in the 1890s by marine contractor John Allmendinger. Sold and remodeled in 1899, the name was changed to the Park Hotel. Dr. Saltzman purchased it in 1905 and remodeled it and changed the name again, adding sixty hotel rooms and a bathhouse with thirty tubs that was finished in white Georgian marble.

The Village Inn in Coloma featured a new band and an entirely different type of floor show that included dancing to Jimmy Foster and his music. There were reduced prices on all drinks and no cover charge.

The Verdemac Tea Room, east of Coloma, featured chicken and steak dinners.

Though the Ellinee Resort is long gone, the sign is now on exhibit at the North Berrien Historical Museum in Coloma, Michigan. *Jane Simon Ammeson*.

Mineral baths were a big draw in the twin cities of St. Joseph and Benton Harbor from the late 1800s to the mid-1950s or so. Pictured here is the Dwan Hotel, which was located in Benton Harbor and advertised that each of its one hundred guest rooms contained every convenience for the public. Patrons could ride elevators up to each floor and make telephone calls from their rooms. The bathhouse featured thirty-two tubs and a special glass called Vitrolite that was used to finish the bathhouse walls and floors. *Benton Harbor Public Library*.

Ice cream was available at this drugstore, which most likely had a soda fountain, as almost all drugstores did in the late 1800s and early 1900s. *St. Joseph Public Library*.

The interior of the Oliver Hotel dining room. *The History Museum*.

SHERIDAN BEACH HOTEL, SHERIDAN BEACH, MICHIGAN CITY, IND.   83728

A view of Michigan City's Sheridan Hotel from the sands of Lake Michigan. *La Porte County Historical Society.*

Dining and dancing at the Red Top Villa on Highland Avenue meant chicken, steak, fish dinners and good entertainment every night by Harvey Cohen, as well as the "The Best Foods—the Finest of Beers."

The Austin Restaurant and Bakery was located in Benton Harbor on what became known as the Austin Block. The restaurant was open from 1896 to the fall of 1907 before changing hands and becoming the tony-sounding Bon Ton Café and Bakery. The Bon Ton proudly announced that it served "the best $0.25 meal in the city."

Violet Joy and Her Orchestra played every evening except Monday, including Sunday afternoon, at the Higman Park Villa (overlooking Lake Michigan and Jean Klock Park), which billed itself as the "Twin Cities' Most Picturesque Resort." Under the management of Fred "Fritz" Drechsel, the villa specialized in fish, steak and chicken dinners at all hours and boasted modern hotel accommodations.

"It is always cool at the Whitcomb Yacht Club. The Whitcomb Hotel's New Air Conditioned Bar, where there was dancing every night both in the main dining room and Yacht Club." Food critic and guidebook writer Duncan Hines visited the Whitcomb Hotel and dined there several times.

The Holiday House was recommended by Duncan Hines, the renowned food critic and restaurant reviewer. The owner was born in Chicago but

Right: The menu cover for the Wigwam, a restaurant with a Native American theme, albeit one more suited for an earlier era, in Dowagiac. *The Dowagiac Area History Museum.*

Below: The Sheridan Hotel in Michigan City was built in 1921. *La Porte County Historical Society.*

119

The Whitcomb Hotel dining room. *St. Joseph Public Library*.

The Holiday House, pictured here in 1955, located at Peach Lane Farms on U.S. 12, two miles south of St. Joseph, was owned and personally operated by Robert and Eleanor Metz. *Jane Simon Ammeson*.

J.L. Sweney, a visitor at the Teegarden House in 1875, wrote the following review in the Plymouth newspaper the *Weekly Republican*: "The Teegarden House is one of the best arranged houses in the State....His tables are well set and furnished with bright silver ware; his eatables are prepared by none but experienced cooks and are served up in any style or manner to suit the taste. His dining room girls are smart...and always ready to await your pleasure, no matter what you call for. His sleeping rooms are splendidly furnished, well ventilated, and always in good order for those who retire to them, in fact they are so neat and handsome that one would think he was entering a parlor. His beds are splendid, better than can be found in any Hotel in the State." *Photograph and information courtesy the LaPorte County Historical Society.*

whose father was a Viennese diplomat, spent a lot of time in Europe, which influenced his culinary outlook.

The Teegarden House, in 1875, was described as having tables that were well set and furnished with bright silverware; meals were prepared by none but experienced cooks and "are served up in any style or manner to suit the taste." One reviewer described it thusly: "The dining room girls are smart… and always ready to await your pleasure, no matter what you call for."

In 1886, the Commercial House in Dowagiac was renovated and began renting rooms for one dollar a night. Meals cost twenty-five cents.

"The Best and Most Magnificent Hotel in Indiana, one of the finest in the United States, and the Best in Any City of 40,000 Inhabitants in the World," is how the Oliver Hotel was described. The Oliver's menu from 1901 lists haunch of venison, Bailey's beaten biscuits, Washington punch and spiced pudding among its offerings.

Hotel Rumely, La Porte, Indiana 81610

Opposite, top: Edward N. Kalamaros opened the Moderne Restaurant on West Washington Street in 1927, adding a distinctive Czechoslovakian stained-glass window over the front entrance. *The History Museum.*

Opposite, bottom: The Redwood Room advertised itself as Indiana's finest supper club, serving high-quality food for lunch and dinner at moderate prices. There was dining and dancing every evening, except Sunday. The Redwood Room was located in Hotel Elkhart in Elkhart, Indiana. *Benton Harbor Public Library.*

Above: A.P. Andrew Jr. made two trips to New York City to help secure funding for an extension of the railroad. The trips, one in 1838 and another the following year, required him to spend two nights and one day on the road from Detroit on Lake Erie to Buffalo and then three days and two nights traveling from Buffalo to Albany, where he had to wait overnight for a steamboat to New York—a ten-hour ride. *Information and photograph courtesy of the LaPorte County Historical Society.*

Located in downtown LaPorte, the Rumely Hotel had one hundred rooms and seventy-five baths and was "air conditioned for your comfort."

The Rumely's Colonial Dining Room and Silver Cocktail Lounge and Bar were, according to its advertising, "Famous for Good Food. U.S."

In 1914, the dining rooms at Palace Buffet on State Street in St. Joseph were roomy and the bar was set up to display all the available spirits, inviting patrons to sit back and enjoy their Blatz beer (fresh from the tap everyday) or something stronger, such as their bonded whiskeys. Oh, and there were cigars to smoke as well.

At the Looking Glass in Dowagiac, the menu included chicken with Champagne sauce, and South Bend Oscar (sole topped with crabmeat,

Rumely Hotel, La Porte, Ind.

Lobby.

Main Dining Room.

While there, Andrew stayed at the Astor House and was so impressed with its food and spirits that he brought back the menu, checking the foods he liked most, including a leg of mutton, turkey and oysters, roast beef and turtle and oysters. The Colonel Restaurant and the Tap Room were located in the Rumely Hotel. *Information and photograph courtesy of the LaPorte County Historical Society.*

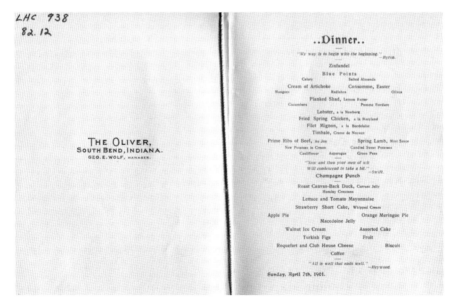

A menu from the Oliver, dated 1901. *The History Museum.*

Your host...

Jim Reynolds
104 Park Place • Dowagiac, Michigan • (616) 782-5600

The Gas Light in Dowagiac. *The Dowagiac Area History Museum.*

asparagus and Hollandaise sauce) and Fish en croute (seasonal fish baked in a golden brown pastry). All dinners included garlic toast and crackers, a gourmet table, tossed salad, a loaf of bread and hot tea and coffee.

At the Brandywine at the LaSalle Hotel in South Bend (built in 1921 and closed in 1973), you could sip such cocktails as pink squirrels, golden Cadillacs, grasshoppers and pink ladies.

At the Gas Light in Dowagiac, one could choose from such selections as Blue Water Lake Perch with French fries and a tossed salad ($2.95); an egg roll with shrimp, cottage cheese and pineapple ($0.65); an eight-ounce Delmonico steak with French fries, a salad and coffee ($5.00); and a hot pastrami sandwich ($2.95). A sloe gin fizz would cost you $1.25, a Singapore sling cost $2.00, a Mogan David Highball cost $1.00 and an orange blossom cost $1.50.

We're trying to figure out why you would name a restaurant in Dowagiac the Ohio Café? Well, no matter. It was a popular place located on Commercial Street. Patrons kept warm with the use of wood burning Round Oak stoves such as an E model with Doe-Wah-Jack finial made between 1905 and 1907. Round Oak Stoves were made in Dowagiac.

The Spaulding Hotel in La Porte had a tank of live lobsters for diners to select from for their meals. The hotel bar was called the Town Club. And the coffee shop was a place where you could get a soft drink and fries.

The Philadelphia, founded in 1901 by Eustice Poledor, along with his brothers Andrew and Pendel, offered a raspberry ice cream soda for fifteen cents, according to a 1930s menu. A chocolate cashew sundae cost twenty cents, as did an egg chocolate milkshake. Sandwiches, soups and salads were also available. The chocolates and candy in display cases were measured and sold by the pound. The candy store, located at 116 North Michigan Street in downtown South Bend, also featured a soda fountain and lunch counter.

The Golden Sands in Michigan City at the Junction of 12 and 212 had a smorgasbord in 1968, while the same year, the L.H. Inn on Lincoln Way East in Mishawaka had a piano bar in the lounge and dancing nightly. Its menu featured seafood and steaks.

Above: The luxurious Spaulding Hotel, with a two-story lobby, was located at the northeast corner of Franklin and Seventh Streets. At the time it was completed in 1922, it was the tallest building in La Porte County. Note the sign for the Spaulding Coffee Shop, which served, besides coffee, colas and fries. The hotel's restaurant had a tank of live lobsters for diners to select from for their meals. The hotel bar was called the Town Club. The hotel also had an illuminated archway entrance. *LaPorte County Historical Society*.

Opposite, top: The Philadelphia, a confectionary, restaurant, soda fountain and bakery located at 116 North Michigan Street in South Bend, was celebrating its thirty-ninth year in business when this photograph was taken in 1940. The candy store also featured a soda fountain and lunch counter. The establishment closed its downtown location in 1972, and the building that housed it was demolished one year later. *The History Museum*.

Opposite, middle: Downtown Dowagiac. Note the drugstore sign advertising a soda fountain. *The Tichnor Brothers Collection, Boston Public Library*,

Opposite, bottom: Pueblo Holiday Inn and Holidome at 444 Pine Lake Avenue in LaPorte. *LaPorte County Historical Society*.

The Ice House in Mishawaka featured a Champagne brunch for $4.94 in 1976 and for their Sunday special, there was chicken coqu au vin with sauteed mushrooms, pearl onions, Parisienne potatoes and buttered broccoli for $3.50.

The Royal Hibernian Room at the Albert Pick Motor Inn at 213 West Washington Street in South Bend had free pakring and a Sunday Brunch for $3.50 in 1976.

Front Street, looking North, Dowagiac, Mich.

LOOKING TO ENTICE BOTH families and businesspeople, Holiday Inn hit on the idea of Holidomes: climate-controlled indoor spaces that saved you the trouble of, say, traveling to New Mexico when you could stay in LaPorte and feel as though you were in the Southwest.

8
UNIQUELY MICHIANA

Quirky advertisements, uniquely designed restaurants, intriguing names and food trends that have come and gone—Michiana had it all.

Chicken-in-the-Rough. Never heard of it? Most people haven't, but at one time, it was bigger than Kentucky Fried Chicken.

It all started back during the Depression, when a down-and-out couple, Beverly and Rubye Osborne, with their life savings gone, were on the road from their home in Oklahoma to California. During the trip, the truck hit a bump, tossing the chicken that Rubye was holding on the floor. She declared, "This is really chicken in the rough." That was enough for her husband, who turned the truck around and headed back home, where they founded Chicken-in-the-Rough, a franchise where franchisees cooked chicken covered with a proprietary blend of spices on a special griddle invented by Osbourne. To fund the business and open a restaurant, Rubye sold her wedding ring. It all worked out. Their fried chicken, served with shoestring potatoes and a hot biscuit with honey, was a huge hit.

It all tied in with the increase of travel and more people eating on the road. Currently, a study by Stanford University indicated more than 20 percent of Americans' meals are eaten in the car. There are currently over 204,000 fast-food restaurants in the United States. These fast-food restaurants serve roughly fifty million Americans every day and bring in $110 billion in annual revenues.

But that wasn't the case in 1936, when Chicken-in-the-Rough got its start. Howard Johnson's was yet to expand like it did in the 1950s, and KFC didn't franchise until 1952.

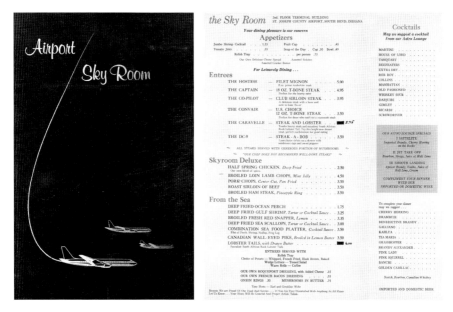

Left: The menu of the Airport Sky Room at the South Bend Airport. *The History Museum.*

Right: The Airport Sky Room was not only a place to get a meal while waiting, but it was also a dining destination. *The History Museum.*

The interior of the dining room. Families were invited to come dine and watch the planes land. *The History Museum.*

Left: The Sky Room offered an extensive menu. *The History Museum.*

Below: South Bend Airport is now the South Bend International Airport. *The History Museum.*

As hard as it is to believe now, cars didn't even have cup holders then. Those didn't come around until 1983, when Chrysler placed built-in cup holders in their minivans. In the 1920s, Model T cup holder attachments could be ordered aftermarket from the *Sears* catalog. You could also get, for your car, kitchenettes, flowerpots and snack trays. In 1957, Cadillac offered a magnetized pull-out bar in the glove compartment of its Eldorado Broughams, but none of these really caught on until the age of minivans.

"HAPPY DAYS! HAPPY DAYS! HERE AT LAST. A CHICKEN DINNER THAT REQUIRES NO SILVERWARE."

With an appetite unbounded, did you ever want to just sit down to a swell chicken dinner, pick up a piece of meat and then start chewing without even going through the formality of using silverware? Well, that opportunity has arrived. Bowman's Restaurant in New Buffalo on US 12 is now featuring chicken dinners with the captivating title "Chicken in the Rough." Served unjointed, without the least semblance of silverware, one simply digs down through the shoestring potatoes in quest of his favorite portion.

THERE ARE ONLY A few Chicken-in-the-Rough restaurants left in the United States—and they're dwindling fast—that still serve chicken in the rough, but back in the middle of the last century, it was a huge hit.

Prior to its name being changed to the Chicken Ranch, the Berghoff, located next to the Caldwell Theater in Saint Joseph, was serving chicken in the rough for fifty cents for one-half chicken. "Every bite a delicious delight," read the tagline of the advertisement. It was served cut up with no utensils, but it did come with gobs of shoestring potatoes, a jug of honey and a hot butter biscuit.

In 1942, the Chicken Ranch at 415 State Street in Saint Joseph featured chicken in the rough, as well as ranchburgers with shoestring potatoes for twenty-five cents. It also offered a complete stock of dry-cooled beer. If you think that, with a name like that, it was some kind of greasy spoon, you'd be wrong. According to the *Herald Press*, proprietors Chester Remus and August Piehl announced the restaurant had undergone extensive remodeling, which included painting the walls in two shades of pink and the ceiling a light ivory color with booths to match. New fluorescent lights were installed, as were Venetian blinds. But the big deal was that the restaurant would be serving chicken in the rough. That, the newspaper article explained, was the nation's current number one eating delight, having made its bow at the café. "This dish is now served in 161 cities in the United States and has proved a sensation at the San Francisco Golden Gate Exposition on Treasure Island," the reporter continued. "The chicken is prepared on a patented griddle and served at the table, counter, in cars at the curb, or in a convenient picnic box that may be taken home or to a party."

In 1943, chicken in the rough was being served at the Caldwell Café, next to the Caldwell Theater in Benton Harbor, and at the Royal Café in Mishawaka, which advertised, "The Original Chicken in the Rough."

TANGERINE

For the enjoyment of our other guests, we ask that you
please refrain from smoking pipes or cigars.

⊗ Appetizers ⊗

BAKED CRABMEAT & SHRIMP	$4.75
Creamed & Sherried with Mushrooms on Half Shell	
SHRIMP COCKTAIL	$6.00
FRESH MUSHROOMS	$4.75
Sauteed in Butter, Garlic & Wine	
AVOCADO CRABMEAT COCKTAIL In Season	$5.25
ESCARGOTS Baked in Shallot Butter	$4.75
FETTUCINI ALFREDO	$5.00
An Italian Classic - Egg Noodles in a Sauce of Cream, Butter and Aged Parmesan and Romano Cheese.	
BAKED BRIE	$6.00
Baked in a pastry puff until golden brown. Served with bread and fresh fruit	
SCAMPI	$6.00
Sauteed in butter & garlic.	

⊗ Soups ⊗

BAKED FRENCH ONION SOUP	$3.00
SOUP DU JOUR	$2.25

⊗ A La Carte Salads ⊗

SPINACH SALAD	$4.75
AVOCADO SALAD In Season	$5.00
CAESAR'S SALAD	$4.75

⊗ A La Carte Vegetables ⊗

SAUTEED ZUCCHINI PROVENCAL	$3.75
"A Vegetarian's Dream". Sauteed zucchini, mushrooms sweet peppers, onions, tomatoes provencal	
STUFFED BAKED POTATO	$2.25
VEGETABLE DU JOUR	$2.50

Appetizers at Tangerine ran the gamut from escargots in shallot butter for $4.75 to baked brie in puff pastry for $6.00. *La Porte County Historical Society*.

On September 21, 1948, Joe Nabicht's Restaurant at 213 Main Street in South Bend promised diners chicken in the rough with "gobs of shoestring potatoes and a jug of honey," along with steaks, seafood, chops and roasts.

In 1950, Lake Shore Tavern on Paw Paw Lake in Coloma featured Les White's Polka Band, sandwiches of all kinds and beer and wine, dancing every Saturday night and chicken in the rough.

In December 1960, the Main Restaurant in South Bend was offering chicken in the rough for one dollar, an offer that expired with the coming new year.

Rouch's Eating House announced a discount for its chicken in the rough. Its regular price of $1.39, which got customers five pieces of pan-fried chicken, a large serving of shoestring potatoes and two hot buttered rolls with special honey, was reduced to $1.00. The advertisement, which ran in the *South Bend Tribune* on July 18, 1966, called it the world's most famous chicken dish. Since the dish was cooked to order, diners were encouraged to call ahead fifteen minutes so they didn't have to wait.

Ervin's Duck Inn on Ford and Warren Street featured pierogi on Friday night and chicken in the rough from five o'clock in the afternoon to midnight on Saturday.

THE COLONEL COMES TO TOWN

Howell's in Plymouth offered "The Original Chicken in the Rough" at reasonable prices, according to an advertisement in 1941, along with roasts, ham, steaks and turkey.

That all changed when Barbara Ann Schori, with her husband, Robert bought Howell's, according to her obituary, became a franchisee of Kentucky Fried Chicken in 1958. They were paid a personal visit by Colonel Sanders, who persuaded them. The couple went on to own five KFC restaurants, including one in Warsaw, Indiana.

LEICESTERSHIRE SAUCE?

When it came to meals served at the resorts, they were usually served in what was known as American style: a fixed price served at specific times. At the Forest Hall Resort on Sister Lakes, orders requested but not on the bill of fare cost extra, but diners certainly had a wide range of choices, such as black and green tea or coffee, plain bread, French rolls, Graham bread, buttered toast or dry toast and a selection of cold meats, including ham salad, lamb, veal, roast beef, tongue and pressed corned beef. French mustard, chow chow, cucumber pickles, slaw, tomato catsup and Halford Sauce were among the relishes offered. In case you're wondering, Halford sauce, also known as Leicestershire sauce, was once as popular as ketchup but is no longer manufactured. From Leicestershire, England, it's comparable to Worcestershire sauce. Then there were sirloin steaks, veal cutlets, bacon and lamb chops to choose from, followed by the option of three potatoes, baked, stewed and pan-fried, with fruit and cake for dessert.

While Leicestershire sauce and chicken in the rough didn't make it, other Michiana foods did.

BAR-SCHEEZE

Probably the biggest breakout food product associated with a local restaurant—albeit one that started off in Marshall, Michigan—was Win Schuler's bar cheese. It was introduced in 1952 and then known as bar-scheeze. Schuler's first opened in Marshall in 1909, and by the mid-1900s, it had several locations, including one in Jackson and, in 1954, Saint Joseph.

Now, if you're like me when you read this, you're thinking, "Oh, that's wrong. Win Schuler's was in Stevensville." And you'd be right. But it turns out that about a decade after opening in Saint Joseph, the restaurant caught on fire, and though firefighters used forty-nine thousand gallons of water while attempting to put out the flames (they even drained the pool at the Snowflake Motel, which was across the highway), nothing was left but ashes. Photographs in the July 8, 1963 issue of the *Herald Press* show how smoke obscured parts of Schuler's Fireside Lounge so that it reads "Schulers Fires." The new Schuler's was built the following year, farther south on Red Arrow Highway, though it, too, was recently torn down to make way for a car wash.

All of the Schuler's are now gone, except for the original in Marshall. And you can still buy Schuler's bar cheese as well.

The unique Snow Flake Motel and Lounge in St. Joseph, Michigan, was built by a Frank Lloyd Wright protégé and was listed in the register of National Historic Places. Built around a center court, its hexagon shape was extremely unique. It had a restaurant, coffee shop, cocktail lounge, banquet room and luxurious amenities. *St. Joseph Public Library.*

The Benton Harbor Fruit Market was once the largest of its kind in the world and attracted not only farmers but visitors as well. *The Tichnor Brothers Collection, Boston Public Library.*

PIZZA HAS ROOTS IN Gary, Indiana. Yes, really. It was back in the 1940s at the Flamingo in downtown Gary where Gus Romeo began making pizza pies. Now, Gary isn't in Michiana, it's near Chicago in a region called Northwest Indiana, but Romeo had several people working for him, and they turned pizza making into a show. Standing in front of a large window, they tossed the dough around while twirling it around. What can we say? People lined up to watch. Remember, television was still very new back then, and though the number of homes owning sets had increased from 6,000 in 1946 to 12 million in 1951, that still was a relatively small number. Currently, there's an estimated 123.8 million TV sets in the United States.

Ten years later, in 1951, *Colliers* magazine wrote a story about this new food trend and featured the Flamingo with a handful of other restaurants across the country as among the few making pizza pies (that's what they called them). Romeo suggested to his cousin Nick Barcevic Sr. that he should open a Flamingo in South Bend. It sounded like a good idea, but there was already a little bar in the city called the Flamingo. Nick's son Nick Jr., who also worked at the Flamingo, was fifteen at the time, and he told me this when I interviewed him for *Edible Michiana* magazine. So, they named their place the Volcano instead.

"Pizza was new back then; I think Gus had the first pizza place in the state," said Barcevic, now eighty-four, who owns the Volcano with his son Jerrod. "We would dress in chefs' hats and make pizza in the front window, and people would come and watch us tossing the dough into the air and catching it. They'd never seen anything like it."

The restaurant started in downtown South Bend, and it is still in business but was moved out by the South Bend International Airport in 1987. But it still uses many of Romeo's original recipes.

As for the Flamingo, it, too, relocated in the mid-1970s to Miller Beach, an eclectic enclave of bungalows, Mid-Century Modern homes and mega-houses on the shores of Lake Michigan.

REALLY? ODD GIVEAWAYS AND ADVERTISEMENTS

In 1966, Nicola's at 607 North Michigan Street in South Bend celebrated its eighth anniversary by giving out a free pair of nylons with an order of one of its large pizzas.

Dog 'n Suds in South Bend, Michigan. *The History Museum.*

"A REAL WIFESAVER" is what the advertisement for the Volcano Restaurant read in the July 23, 1954 edition of the *South Bend Tribune*. What's with those Italian places? Nylons? Wifesaver? Really?

But the Volcano had somewhat of an explanation that made sense. Back then, over 66 percent of married women didn't work outside of the home, and only one in twenty-two homes had one air conditioner or more (remember, most air conditioners back then were window units), meaning only 4.5% of homes in the United States were air conditioned. When you look at it that way, not firing up the home stove and, instead, going to an air conditioned restaurant would be a treat.

The Temple News Agency, located in the Masonic temple building on Jefferson Avenue in LaPorte, Indiana, closed several years ago, after being a popular favorite for over a century. *La Porte County Historical Society.*

The House of David Service Station. *Benton Harbor Public Library.*

As for the nylons given away at Niocola's?

Well, I don't have an explanation for that.

Most diners expect their food to be served on clean plates, but in 1948, maybe that wasn't something to take for granted. How else to explain the advertisment for Dunham's Snack Bar in Watervliet that not only touted its "New Look" in fountain treats, including super sodas, whipped cream sundaes and extra thick malted. It also touted it had the "Best of Foods, Air Conditioning," and also "Clean Dishes."

In 1954, Smith's Cafeteria in South Bend advertised its tasty food was served piping hot. So many places emphasized warm or hot food, one has to wonder if that was a major concern. I mean, think about it. Can you think of any restaurant today advertising hot food?

The Philadelphia advertised a complete baked sugar-cured ham dinner with all the trimmpings (not sure if that was an error in the advertisement that ran in the *South Bend Tribune* on Saturday, January 21, 1956, or that was a culinary term I've never heard of). Trimmpings or trimmings, the entire meal cost $1.60, and there were special children's portions as well.

Oysters

In the 1800s, oysters were the thing. They were shipped in big barrels from the East Coast by railroad, and everyone seemed to eat them. Now, I love oysters, but a lot of people don't. But that didn't seem to be the case one hundred years or more ago.

Indeed, according to the Friday, July 26, 1907 edition of the *Bristol Banner*, published in Bristol, Indiana, in St. Joseph County, New Yorkers consumed 500,000 bushels of oyster the previous season. A bushel of oysters contains about 200 oysters, so from September 1, 1906, to the end of April 1907, 100 million oysters were devoured by New Yorkers.

In 1855, the Rochester House Saloon in Dowagiac featured oysters, lobsters, pigs' feet, Edinburgh Scotch, Champagne, Madeira pints and sherry, all to be served in "good style." Four years later, Wm. McNab announced that the Rochester House Saloon would be carrying Elliott and Demings Count oysters in kegs, half kegs and cans.

In 1888, Weber's in Saint Joseph advertised Baltimore Oysters as the best bivalves on the market.

F. Vanderhoof ran an advertisement in the *South Bend Tribune* in 1881 that said he "secured the services of Ed Gillen (who had no equal in the handling of oysters)....He will hereafter be found at my place of business, No. 70 Washington Street...and will serve the delicious bivalve in any style. Also for sale by the quart or gallon." In season, the restaurant would also feature fresh shell oysters, clams, lobsters and soft shell crabs.

The Loveridge family, who founded a grocery store in Marcellus in the late 1800s and went on to own the Loveridge Hotel, advertised the daily availability of oysters.

The Minnesota Restaurant on the Kepler block in Benton Harbor served oysters in every style, according to an advertisement in the *Herald Palladium* in 1888.

Robert Westphahl had both a restaurant and an oyster room at 126 South Michigan Avenue in 1889.

In 1900, the Higbee Hotel in Benton Harbor was offering a turkey dinner with oyster dressing on their Thanksgiving menu and chicken pie. They also featured rabbit pot pie, hunter style and oyster stew.

In 1890, the Chicago Restaurant on State Street in St. Joseph advertised oysters as well as steaks and seafood.

Wilson's Bakery and Restaurant on State Street in St. Joseph advertised oysters direct from Baltimore in 1903.

The Hayes Hotel on Fish Lake in Marcellus kept chickens for the freshest of eggs for its guests' breakfasts. Mrs. Hayes cooked and served family-style, like many early lakeside resorts, and, in the 1920s, advertised chicken dinners for twenty-five cents each. *Jane Simon Ammeson.*

Club Lido in South Bend offered both a Chinese and American menu, along with Blue Point and New York oysters, available stewed, fried or raw. It had a large choice of chop suey, chow mein, sub gum and fried rice.

The menu for Sunday, December 31, 1939, to January 1, 1940, at the Chatterbox on Pipestone Avenue listed select oysters with tartar sauce for sixty-five cents and roast young Tom Turkey with oyster dressing for ninety cents. Fried chicken cost ten cents less and prime rib with gravy and lamb chops were seventy cents. The price of the dinner included selections such as shrimp cocktail, whipped potatoes, peas, spiced beets and desserts like mince or pumpkin pie. Interestingly, there still is a Chatterbox in Benton Harbor, but this one is in a different location and doesn't seem to be associated with the original.

Roy E. Shipe was the proprietor at Dwan Coffee Shop in Saint Joseph, where, on Sunday December 11, 1938, menu items included fresh mushroom broth, anchovies, choice of fruit or tomato juice, oyster cocktail. With that you could choose boned roast young turkey, chef's special T-bone steak or filet mignon for seventy-five cents; fried lake trout or grilled pork chops and baked apples for forty-five cents; roast leg of lamb with cranberry sauce, eight fried select oysters, or Chinese chop suey with chow mein noodles and rice for fifty cents; and baked ground round steak and mushrooms for thirty-five cents. These meals also included fresh tomatoes, butter beans, tuna salad, asparagus and potatoes either mashed or fried.

And according to the advertisement, there were "Always—Waffles—Always."

WHO DOESN'T LOVE THE warm, fuzzy feeling of a place that uses the first name of its owner? It's like you could just walk in and be on a first-name basis. Andy's Candy on Jefferson in South Bend. Angelo's Sunset View Motel in Benton Harbor. Arthur's Big Bend Drive-In (Saint Joseph). Bushbaum's was the place to go for lunch. Ben's Grill on Washington Street in South Bend. Butch's Bar in Mishawaka. Charlie's Tavern at 718 West Indiana Street in South Bend.

Don's Bar & Restaurant in Mishawaka offered one-half of a fried chicken with coleslaw, fries, honey and rolls for $1.75 in 1963.

Guys named Ed seemed to own a lot of restaurants. There was Ed's Tavern in Mishawaka, Ed's Grill in Eau Claire and Eddie's, a drive-in, in Coloma. Ed's Café, a family-owned restaurant in Coloma specializing in fried chicken, was in business for more than a half-century.

There was also Elbode's in Mishawaka.

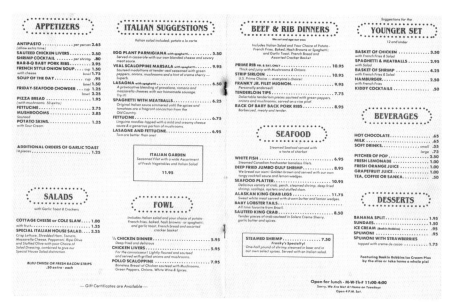

Though it specialized in Italian foods, Franky's in Niles included a wide range of menu offerings. Frank Frucci Jr. owned Franky's for forty-five years before retiring in 1990 and was the creator of what was described as the "World Famous Stacked Ham Sandwich." *The History Museum.*

Flip's and Dale's were both donut shops in Saint Joseph. Flip's was downtown and Dale's was in South Saint Joseph.

Frankie's of South Bend advertised having the best Italian food in town, as well as a large menu of American foods.

The Silver Foam is a wonderful name for a saloon and was located at 116 Territorial. Unfortunately for them, in 1909, thieves stole two dozen whiskey bottles, five hundred cigars and two dozen bottles of beer.

There was Green Lantern Inn in Hartford and a Blue Lantern Inn on Hudson Lake.

Could you possibly be sad at Happy's Bar at 217 South Chapin Street in South Bend?

In the 1940s, Hank's Panel Room next to Hank's Texaco at the Hartford, Michigan exit on Interstate 94 advertised roast chicken dinners every Sunday for $1.50 in its air conditioned dining room. Patrons could also order a sirloin tip steak sandwich for $1.50 or foot-long hotdogs, and the Friday Special was all-you-can eat fresh lake perch. The restaurant also featured a self-service drive-thru. It is still in business in the same location, but it is now known as the Panel Room.

Chief's Bar & Grill in Millburg north of Benton Harbor has been owned by the same family since 1948. Get there early on Thursday night for their prime rib special.

In 1950, Harvey's, located four miles south of Saint Joseph, had a main dining room, as well as two private dining rooms and a cocktail lounge, and served chicken, steak and seafood dinners.

In the 1950s, both Harvey's Department Store and Woolworth's in Dowagiac featured dining counters.

In 1963, Hawley's Restaurant was the place for a Coke and French fries with gravy.

Imagine telling people you were going to Babe's, the name of a lounge still in business after over sixty years on the river in Benton Harbor.

Young's Tavern in Benton Harbor became the Farmer's Country Club in the mid-1960s. It remains open today.

According to its website, Henry's Hamburgers, in the early 1960s, had over two hundred locations from coast to coast, which was more stores than McDonald's had at the time. Headquartered in Chicago, only one Henry's

Black Bird Waterhouse in Coloma is located in the renovated Will-O-Paw, a restaurant and gas station dating to the 1920s. *Jane Simon Ammeson.*

remains, and that's the one in the Fairplain section of Benton Harbor that opened in 1959. At first, it was strictly a carryout business until the addition of a drive-thru service in 1988, which now accounts for over 70 percent of sales. Dine-in is also available. In 1970, Henry's advertised a hamburger, French fries and a Coke for fifty-two cents.

The Club Restaurant in Benton Harbor became the Esquire Lounge in 1947 and continued to operate under that name until the late 1970s.

Hill's Hamburger was located on Colfax in South Bend. There was Joe's Inn at 209 Dixie Way in South Bend and John's at 2138 West Washington Street in South Bend.

You could get a complete dinner for $1.00, a special steak dinner for $1.35, all-you-can-eat perch on Friday for $1.00 and luncheons served all day priced at $0.75 to $0.90 until closing at Kitchenette Restaurant on Main Street.

In 1950, Lil and Min's at 198 Pipestone in Benton Harbor wanted you to be sure to order its hoagie sandwiches. "They are delicious."

There was Louie's Bar in New Carlisle, Indiana, that had a location in Benton Harbor as well.

Mike Williamowski owned Tom's Restaurant on Lafayette Boulevard in downtown South Bend. We think it was a good idea he didn't call his place Williamowski's.

Mikey's Drive-In in Bridgman, which specializes in made-to-order hamburgers, a variety of fries, ice cream and malts, was once Had's Drive-In. Built in 1950, it's been Mikey's for more than three decades.

The Miller family owned Miller's Home Café in New Carlisle for fifty-seven years, closing its doors in 2017. They had a buffet and advertised a smorgasbord in 1968.

Milt's Grill on Main Street in Colfax offered diners free drinks and fries if they bought a basket burger in 1945. That same offer was given in 1954, only customers weren't given fries; instead, they could get a shake, malt or other drink.

You could dine and dance all day and night at Paul's Dine and Dance on the Water at the Sister Lakes.

There were two places named Ramona, a dance hall on the Sister Lakes and the bar at 1653 East Fourth Street in Mishawaka. In 1945, the bar had a fish fry every Friday and spaghetti dinners every Saturday night.

Fish fries were popular, and the Red Coach in Stevensville had one every Friday night as well as chicken dinners on Sunday in 1968. The restaurant is gone now, but there is a Red Coach Donut Shop in Stevensville. That same

D'Agostino's Navajo Bar and Grill dates to 1932, when it was the Navajo Trading Company, and it featured a zoo with wild animals. Now it's a supper club–style restaurant. *Jane Simon Ammeson.*

St. Julian Winery, the oldest winery in the state, has also won the most awards of any winery in Michigan and was the first to have a woman winemaker. *St. Julian Winery.*

year, the Sunday special was chicken and dumplings at Eagle Park Inn on Eagle Lake in Edwardsburg.

Sally Swiss Buffet in South Bend also offered a smorgasbord.

Tom's Café at 2208 Mishawaka Avenue in South Bend announced that, beginning Sunday, January 22, 1956, it would be open on Sundays for home-cooked dinners, such as barbecue ribs and whole barbecue chicken.

There was Walt's Ideal Bar in Benton Harbor and Walt's Drive-In, which was open twenty-four hours a day. Located on Michigan Street in South Bend, it advertised "Famous for Food, Dining Room and Coffee Shop."

Was the White Front Tavern at 1302 Prairie Street in South Bend painted white? Speaking of white, while it was nicknamed Fat Shirley's, its official name was the White House Restaurant in South Bend. It was a twenty-four-hour diner where even the bacon was said to be cooked in butter. Back in the day, the truckers' special, which included three eggs, toast, bacon and home fries, would set you back four dollars and add up to who knows how many calories.

There was also Wilbur's Ice Cream in Saint Joseph.

Other names we like in South Bend are Wade's, Ollie's, Stanley's Tavern and Rocco's.

Owners Behaving Badly

Breach of Promise

When Nick's Hotel in Benton Harbor opened on September 22, 1923, several thousand people showed up to inspect one of the most modern hostelries in the city. There were souvenirs for everyone who attended, according to the *Herald Palladium*; carnations were given to the ladies, and cigars distributed to the men. While the guests were escorted through the hotel to visit the billiard room and the lunch counter, the House of David twelve-piece orchestra played.

Two years later, owner Nicholas Dorotheou got into a little trouble when Antonia Moutatson sued him for $25,000 after he reneged on his promise to marry her. Antonia was the niece of Andrew Moutastson, the owner of the Palace of Sweet at Main and Pipestone Streets. Mr. Dorotheou and Mr. Moutastson were described by the newspaper as two of the best-known and wealthiest Greek men in the area. Miss Moutastson, twenty-two, who resided in Sault Ste. Marie, said she and Mr. Dorotheou had become acquainted

Hotel Michigan and Nick's Restaurant in downtown Benton Harbor. *St. Joseph Public Library.*

when she visited her uncle, and their engagement was later announced at a function attended by many prominent Greek people at the Emery Resort. Several wedding dates were set, but the groom-to-be kept postponing the ceremony. There were letters that her attorney said he would introduce into evidence. Mr. Dorotheou indicated he would fight the case. We don't know if Antonia got her money, but we're happy to report that two years later, she married John G. Kovel, had two daughters and died just short of her eighty-eighth birthday.

Tony Barrett and the Owl

The discarded wife dressed in a threadbare coat and living in a small cottage. The glamorous mistress swathed in fine clothes, furs and jewels. Her lover—and the wife's husband—resided in a grand house at 619 South Michigan. Those were parts of the story told when Ollie Barrett sued her husband, John C. Barrett (better known as Tony), for support.

Barrett might have done better to pay his wife rather than let it go to court. Why he didn't might reflect his long history of breaking the law and getting away with it. Whenever there was a raid, there often was a phone call made before the cops came bursting in. It gave him time enough to hide the cards, the roulette wheels and the booze when Prohibition was in effect.

It would take hours to catalog all of Tony's arrests and lawsuits, but here are a few, just to give you an idea. On November 13, 1894, a raid of Barrett's place, conducted by Captain Cassidy, led to the discovery of a slot machine, which was confiscated. Barrett and two customers, one a professional man, were arrested. But not to worry about poor Tony going to jail. It seems that no matter how many times Barrett was arrested, he somehow got out of spending too much time in jail.

In a May 10, 1901 article, the *South Bend Tribune* reported Tony faced two different charges of selling liquor on a Sunday and running a gambling operation.

In 1909, Charles Calhoun, who lost $475 at an establishment owned by Barrett, filed suit and asked the court to order a judgment of $500 to compensate for his losses playing roulette. He was also sued in 1935, when operating the German Village Café on Center Street by Morris D. Feldman, who wanted his bar, chairs, tables and other furnishings back, as well as $1,000 in damages.

Ollie again filed for maintenance in 1910, asking for $2,000 a month— not bad for today and a fortune back then.

But let's start at the beginning.

Born into a good family, Tony's father was a jeweler who had a store on North Michigan Avenue. He was described as being a pillar of the first Methodist Episcopal church and the first worshipful master of South Bend Lodge No. 294, F&AM. Tony didn't follow in such august footsteps.

Tony got his start working for Bill Mason, the one-time proprietor of the Sheridan Hotel, and following that, he opened the Gold Gate Saloon in 1886. Thirteen years and other business ventures later, he opened the Owl Saloon in 1889 in a building that had been a livery stable. At the grand opening, visitors were awed by the four fifty-dollar gold pieces embedded in the mosaic floor of the barroom. Forming a square, at each point of the triangle pattern were twenty-dollar gold pieces, covering much of the floor. Then there was the mahogany bar and the mirrored walls and the fine crystal glasses. In other words, this was a place of class, not just any old tavern and gambling den.

But while he may have been smart about his business empire, Tony should have paid more attention to keeping his wife happy—or at least quiet. In 1921, his wife, Ollie Barrett, sued him for support. It seems that she wasn't too happy that a woman she claimed was her husband's favorite mistress, a Mrs. D.A. Livingston, was living with him in a grand house at 619 South Michigan Street while she was living in a small cottage at 112 West Marion Street. In case one didn't know the neighborhoods, the newspaper was kind enough to show photographs of both places. I totally get Mrs. Barrett's point and that wasn't all. There are references to Mrs. Livingston being swathed in furs and silks from the most high-end stores in South Bend, while Ollie struggled to pay her bills, wore a cloth cape coat purchased at a marked-down rate, an inexpensive blue coat suit and a serge dress both bought on sales days.

Though Tony's lawyer admitted that maybe the feed stores he owned were unremunerative (after all, cars were replacing horses, so there was less need for animal feed in a city like South Bend), any allowance should be made on the profits from his real business rather than on balance sheets of the enterprise conducted as a screen.

I'm not sure that was a good strategy, and Judge Fred C. Klein didn't think it was either. It could also be that Ollie's story of having her nephew help her buy a vacuum sweeper on time while her husband contacted the stores and told them not to extend credit to her on his accounts had an impact on the judge as well.

He was probably thinking that Mrs. Livingston didn't seem to have problems getting money from Tony for fine clothes while living a grand life. But I hope Mrs. L. had a back-up plan, because according to Ollie, she was one of more than ten mistresses. Tony was obviously easily bored.

It was unfortunate for Tony that his wife knew so much about his business, and one wonders why he didn't just give her money to make this big mess go away rather than have it published in the papers.

First of all, her lawyers told the court that Tony's wealth might be as high as $1 million. He certainly lived a lavish lifestyle fueled by liquor sales (this was Prohibition) and gambling joints. The liquor, Ollie said, was hidden throughout the county in barns and fields.

Ollie wanted $2000 a month in temporary allowances and fees and $25,000 to pay her attorneys.

Now, you need to pause here and think about this. We are talking about South Bend, Indiana, in 1921. Nationwide, according to government statistics, the average salary per year was approximately $3,400, or over $80,000 a year today ($2,000 then was equivalent to about $67,000 today, give or take a few cents). That would be enough to ensure that Ollie didn't have to shop sales anymore.

The amount Ollie wanted for her attorney fees in response to her husband saying he would spend $50,000 fighting the case, $25,000, is equivalent to $416,215.08 today.

In other words, Ollie was out for blood, and she had the goods.

She didn't get everything she wanted, but Judge Klein awarded Ollie $300 ($5,113.56 today) a month for temporary support until her hearing for separate maintenance, which was set for that August. Her attorneys were granted $2,000, which Tony's lawyers said was way too much for him to come up with. Ollie's lawyer, John G. Yeagley, answered that "a couple of thousand or so does not seem to be a large amount to a man who buys several high-priced automobiles in a year."

Unsurprisingly, Tony didn't pay the lawyers in a timely manner as he was ordered and was able to get an extension of the case, so nothing happened in August. By December, it was still pending.

After that, except for a brief mention that a trial was still pending the following year, the case disappears from the news. Tony probably decided to pay up.

The administration building at the House of David. *St. Joseph Public Library*.

But there was more trouble coming.

In 1926, Tony left town quickly after receiving a tip from a friend on the South Bend Police Force that his place on the third floor of the Crescent Hotel at 121 North Michigan Avenue was about to be raided. While Tony was on his way to Miami, Florida, the police found evidence of a widespread operation he had with booking agents in Marion, Logansport, Fort Wayne and Elkhart, Indiana. In all, just on the business alone, Tony was making thousands of dollars a month—and that was just one facet of his gambling empire. It seems Tony was high tech and connected by a special long-distance telephone to Mont Tennes, a gentleman gambler headquartered in Chicago, and he received reports on races in Tijuana, Mexico; Havana, Cuba; and New Orleans, as well as other places.

He was, in other words, well connected when it came to friends on the force and to a vast gambling empire, but he never spent much time in jail. Indeed, in his spare time, he bought and sold expensive racehorses and spent time at the track.

After the bust in 1926, the police vowed to put Tony out of business.

But that didn't seem to go well, because in 1939, the Owl was still in business, and Tony was still running it. Despite Tony's numerous arrests and proclivities for running gambling dens, when he died at the age of eighty, the *South Bend Tribune* memorialized his life in a long obituary.

As for who got all his money, it didn't say.

King Wurtz

In 1913, King Wurtz (what a wonderful name) testified for Ida V. Moss in the divorce suit she filed against her husband, Thomas M. Moss, the proprietor of the Indiana, American and Majestic Scenic Theaters.

Mrs. Moss, claimed her husband, went to "questionable places" with other men and women, including Grove Willard, King Wurtz and Bert White. But Wurtz, who said he was general manager for Tony Barrett's, which he said was the "most notorious place in the city for gambling," claimed that Mrs. Moss never did anything improper when she and her friends were together. Though examination did find that Mrs. Moss, along with several men and women, while at Harvey Ort's, started on bottled beer and began ordering quarts for at least the first round. This was shocking to say the least.

This wasn't a Sunday school crowd to give you an idea of the type of friends and employees Tony had. Ort, who owned the Grand Saloon and the Nickel Hotel, had been arrested for just about everything. (In an interesting aside, in 1911, Ort sold the Nickel Hotel to a man who claimed to be William Hill. That is until Mrs. Parkin (as Mr. Hill's real name was Parkin) came to town and said it was her money that helped fund the purchase of the hotel and that the woman who claimed to be Mrs. Hill was not his wife. The judge agreed, and she got her money from the trust company where her husband had funds on deposit. Mr. Parkin had already hastily departed town.)

Mr. Moss countered that his wife once knocked out his front tooth in a fight and that she attacked a woman named Nellie Niles and Moss had to pay her off. Nellie, Mrs. Moss claimed, worked for her husband, and the two had "improper" relations."

FROG LEGS MEUNIERE	$11.95
Sauteed in browned lemon butter with shallot	
PORK RIBS	$11.95
Meaty N' tender, baked in our own special sauce.	MARKET
LAMB CHOPS	PRICE
"A Tangerine Favorite". Served with a mint sauce.	

⌁ Fowl ⌁

ROAST DUCK A'L' ORANGE	$14.95
Crisp roast duck, topped with orange sauce.	
CHICKEN BREAST A LA KIEV	$11.95
Crisp on the outside, tender & juicy inside, topped with white grapes.	
CHICKEN RATATOUILLE	$12.95
Plump & tender chicken served on a bed of gently sauteed zucchini, mushrooms, sweet peppers, onions & tomatoes provencal.	
CHICKEN MARSALA	$12.95
Chicken breast sauteed in mushrooms and marsala wine, served with Tangerine rice.	

⌁ Beef ⌁

BEEF WELLINGTON, SAUCE DUXELLE	$16.95
Tender filet wrapped in puff pastry with a hint of pate'.	
PRIME RIB AU JUS	$16.95
Served with creamy horseradish sauce.	
PETITE CUT	$14.95
FILET MIGNON, SAUCE BERNAISE	$16.95
Served with sauteed mushrooms	
PETITE CUT	$14.95
NEW YORK STRIP	$16.95
Succulent sirloin, smothered with sauteed mushrooms	
BROILED SIRLOIN KABOB	$13.95
Skewered sirloin tips with sweet peppers, onions, bacon, tomatoes & mushrooms.	

⌁ Veal ⌁

VEAL PICCATA	$15.95
Tender veal scallops, sauteed in garlic butter & herbed lemon sauce.	
VEAL OSCAR	$16.95
Tender veal, sauteed in butter & topped with asparagus spears, crabmeat & our very special bearnaise sauce.	

APPETIZERS		
	Crab Claw Cocktail	5.50
	Shrimp Cocktail	4.75
	Herring in Wine or Sour Cream	2.95
	Fried Mushrooms . . . 3.50 Half Order	1.95
	Garlic Bread	2.50
	Heston Combo . . . . . fried peppers, zucchini and cauliflower	3.50

ENTREES

SPECIALTY OF THE HOUSE
Prime Rib of Beef, Au Jus

MODEST CUT,	14 oz.	11.95
HOUSE CUT,	22 oz.	16.75
MIKE'S CUT,	36 - 40 oz.	25.50

SERVED WITH HORSERADISH SAUCE
Our Prime Rib is slowly prepared for hours. Please Do Not Be Upset if we occasionally run out.
COMPLETE DINNER - No Sharing Please!

SAUTEED VEAL, tender sliced, lemon butter, mushrooms	11.95
CENTER CUT LAMB CHOPS, 2 - 10 oz. chops, mint jelly	14.95
CENTER CUT PORK CHOPS, 2 - 10 oz. chops, applesauce	9.50
CHOP COMBO, a pork and lamb chop	11.95
FILET MIGNON, sauteed mushrooms	
King Size, 11 oz.	15.95
Queen Size, 7 oz.	10.95
NEW YORK STRIP STEAK, sauteed mushrooms	
King Size, 18 oz.	15.95
Junior Size, 12 oz.	10.95
RIB EYE STEAK, 14 oz., sauteed mushrooms	12.95
BARBECUED BACK RIBS, broiled in our own tangy sauce	9.75
Double Portion	16.50
CHICKEN KIEV, breast of chicken stuffed with herb butter, white wine and sour cream sauce, served on a bed of rice	8.50
BEEF KABOB, beef tenderloin, marinated in our secret oils served on a bed of rice	9.50
BABY BEEF LIVER, sauteed in butter and onions	7.50

All Entrees served with Cheese and Crackers, Soup or Juice, Salad, Choice of Potato or Vegetable, Rolls and Coffee or Hot Tea
EXTRA SETTINGS.....CHILDREN $1.50 ADULTS $2.50
Our Chef Is Not Responsible For The Tenderness Of Steaks Over Medium

Left: The entrées at Tangerine had a definite French flair, with frog legs meuniere ($11.95), roast duck à l'orange ($14.95) and veal Oscar (veal topped with asparagus, crabmeat and béarnaise sauce). *La Porte County Historical Society.*

Right: The specialty of the Heston Supper Club continues to be prime rib. *The History Museum.*

For his part Moss—aside from it being revealed that he kept slot machines in his place of business—said he gave his wife diamond rings and cars. In other words, why couldn't she overlook a girlfriend or two?

The judge ruled in favor of Mrs. Moss after she gave testimony that her husband had beat her, was cruel, came home late and was involved with other women. Mrs. Moss received her divorce as well as $3,500 in alimony and some additional money. Earlier, to keep her from divorcing him in 1908, after she discovered his affair with Nellie Niles, her husband had deeded her the Scenic Theater in South Bend.

It seems it worked out okay for her in the end.

Now that we've talked about the bad boys, let's remember a good gal.

Annie Rinks owned an immaculately clean restaurant at 514 Broad Street (it was across the street from where Rybelle's restaurant is now) called the Green Cow. And no, we don't know where the name came from, but it was a popular place near city hall and the police and fire stations. So, when, after working in restaurants since 1923 and owning the Green Cow for almost twenty-three years, she decided to retire, Tom Gillespie, the chief of police at the time (the year was 1974), organized a farewell party. After all, many of the city's leaders had coffee at the Green Cow in the morning, and she would be missed.

At the age of sixty-eight, Annie was looking forward to retirement, even if her clientele wasn't. After all, it meant she no longer had to get up a 4:00 a.m. and open her doors a 6:00 a.m. "I can go when I want and come when I want," she told the reporter from the *Herald Palladium*. "I've enjoyed every minute of it. There has been more good than bad."

BIBLIOGRAPHY

Ballard, Ralph. *Tales of Early Niles*. Niles, MI: Niles Printing Co., 1946.

Beber, L. Benjamin. *History of Saint Joseph*. St. Joseph, MI: Published under the auspices of Saint Joseph Chamber of Commerce, 1927.

Centennial Book Commemorating the Establishment of a Post Office at Eau Claire, Michigan, on November 7, 1861. Eau Claire, MI: n.p., 1961.

Champion, Ella. *Berrien's Beginnings*. Niles, MI: Trust Department of the First National Bank of Southwestern Michigan, 1926.

Clark, Charles F., Henry H. Chapin, James Edmund Scripps and R.L. Polk. *Michigan State Gazetteer and Business Directory*. Detroit, MI: C.F. Clark, 1856.

Critchley, David. "The American Mafia: The History of Organized Crime in the United States: Gangsters in Southwest Michigan." https://mafiahistory.us/a017/f_swmichigan.html.

Destination Yesterday: Memories and Tales of the Early Twentieth Century in Central Berrien County as Told by Her Senior Citizens. Berrien Springs, MI: Berrien Springs Sesquicentennial, 1981.

Eisenhart, Gladys Roe. *The Story of Scottsdale*. St. Joseph, MI: Class of 1950 Saint Joseph High School, 1975.

Graves, W.W. *Atlas of Berrien County, Michigan*. Chicago: Rand McNally and Company, 1887.

Jumika, Andrea. "Gangsters in Southwest Michigan." The American Mafia. January 31, 2020. https://www.onewal.com/gangsters-in-southwest-michigan/.

King, Sidney J. *King's Routes of Michigan, Province, Ontario, Canada, and New York: A Tour Book of the Principal Automobile Routes in the States of America*. Chicago: n.p., 1913.

Leeper, David Rohrer. *Early Inns and Taverns of South Bend, Indiana, 1832–1900*. South Bend, IN: Helen Hibberd Dwindle, 1943.

Lowry, Wanda. *Bridgeman, Lake Township: The First 100 Years, 1856–1956*. Bridgman, MI: Bridgman–Lake Township Historical Society, 2005.

Myers, Robert C. *Greetings from Benton Harbor*. Historic Photo Book Series. Berrien Springs, MI: Berrien County Historical Association, 2011.

———. *Greetings from Saint Joseph*. Historic Photo Book Series. Berrien Springs, MI: Berrien County Historical Association, 2008.

Poole, Charlotte, and Richard Judd Jr. "This is Magician Lake." https://www.magicianlake.org/magicianlake.org.

Rasmussen, R.L. *Paw Paw Lake: A One Hundred Year Resort History 1890s–1990s*. Dowagiac, MI: Southwestern Michigan Publications, 1994.

———. *Sister Lakes*. Charleston, SC: Arcadia Publishing, 2007.

Thomopoulos, Elaine Cotsirilos, PhD. *Resorts of Berrien County*. Charleston, SC: Arcadia Publishing, 2005.

Tourist Guide of Dowagiac, Michigan—107 Lakes—2,500 Cottages—75 Hotels—the Playground of Southern Michigan. Niles, MI: Leader Publications, April 3, 2007.

Waterman, Alfred Matthews. *History of Cass County, Michigan*. Chicago: Watkins, 1882.

NEWSPAPERS

Dowagiac Daily News
Dowagiac Republican
Edwardsburg Argus
Evening Herald
Herald Argus
Herald Palladium
Herald-Press
La Porte Herald
La Porte Weekly Herald
News-Dispatch (Michigan City)
South Bend Tribune
St. Joseph Weekly Herald
Tri-City Record

WEBSITES

Ancestry. www.ancestry.com.

Berger, Karen, PharmD. "Soda Fountains and Their Pharmacist Inventors." *Pharmacy Times*, February 16, 2019. https://www.pharmacytimes.com/view/soda-fountains--their-pharmacist-inventors.

City By the Lake. http://www.citybythelake.org/forums/lofiversion/index.php.

Genealogy Trails. www.genealogytrails.com.

Internet Archive. "Inventory of the County Archives of Indiana, No. 46, La Porte, Indiana Historical Bureau, Indianapolis, 1939." https://archive.org/details/inventoryofcount02hist.

Library of Congress. https://www.loc.gov.

New Buffalo Township. "History." https://newbuffalotownship.org/about/history.

NewspaperArchive. www.newspaperarchive.com.

Newspapers.com. www.newspapers.com.

PocketSights. https://pocketsights.com/.

Rootsweb. https://sites.rootsweb.com/~inl.../histories/Stage_Coach.html.

Soderlund Drugstore Museum. "History of the Soda Fountain." http://drugstoremuseum.org/index.php/soda-fountain/soda-fountain-history.

ABOUT THE AUTHOR

Jane Simon Ammeson is a freelance writer and photographer who specializes in travel, food, books, personalities and lifestyles. A judge for the James Beard Awards and a Taste Awards Citizen judge, she is the author of seventeen books specializing in travel, historic true crime, history and food. She also writes a weekly book column for the *Northwest Indiana Times* and a food column for the *Herald Palladium*. She is the editor of the Midwest Travel Journalist's newsletter, has contributed to *USA Today*'s "Best of" series and has two blogs, janeammeson.com (about food and travel) and shelflife. blog (features interviews with authors and book reviews). She is also a book reviewer for the *New York Journal of Books*.

Her book *Lincoln Road Trips* won the Bronze Award in the Lowell Thomas Journalism Awards for "Best Travel Book." She blogs about food, wine, culture, history and travel. She currently has over 285,000 visitors to her blog annually. She has written for several travel apps, including Indiana's Best. Her book *Hauntings of the Underground Railroad: Ghosts of the Midwest* was a *Forward Review* Indies finalist.

Visit us at
www.historypress.com